Unplanning

Livable Cities and Political Choices

by

Charles Siegel

Dedicated to Ivan Illich

Cover: Demolition of San Francisco's Central Freeway
Photograph by Charles Siegel

ISBN 978-0-9788728-5-4
Copyright © 2010 by Charles Siegel.
Published by the Preservation Institute, Berkeley, California.
www.preservenet.com

Contents

Chapter 1
Planning and Politics

Environmentalists have not moved beyond the modernist faith in city planning. They say that our cities' environmental problems are caused by lack of planning. When they see problems that were obviously caused by planning, they blame them on insufficient planning – on "piecemeal planning" that looked at transportation or at zoning in isolation. Instead, they say, we need comprehensive regional land-use and transportation planning: if a single agency controlled land-use planning and transportation planning for an entire metropolitan region, it could concentrate new development near transit stations in order to stop sprawl and reduce automobile dependency.

Conservatives attack this sort of comprehensive planning on the grounds that it reduces freedom of choice and that it would replace local decision making with centralized decision making by technocratic planners. Environmentalists have a hard time convincing the public to let the planners make decisions that now are made by individuals and by local government.

The Failures of Planning

Yet environmentalists want more urban planning in order to undo problems caused by modernist urban planning.

Environmentalists want to build cities with walkable, transit-oriented neighborhoods – cities designed like American cities were a century ago, before most people ever heard of city planning. The traditional neighborhoods that environmentalists admire were designed in a piecemeal way. The city laid out the street grid, and then small developers filled in the land uses one at a time. There was little or no land use planning, and there was certainly no centralized coordination of land use and transportation planning.

Early in the twentieth century, the inventors of city planning claimed that this sort of piecemeal development was no longer appropriate in modern cities. These early planners believed that, because the modern technological economy was becoming increasingly centralized, it was inevitable that land uses would be developed on a large-scale and that each would be planned by experts. Just as industrial engineers designed large factory complexes, city planners would design housing developments, office developments, recreational developments, and other land uses on a large scale. All this planning of individual land uses would be controlled by master planning, which would coordinate the location of the different land uses and would ensure that there was adequate transportation for them.

The ideas of the early planners failed when they were put into practice in postwar America. Postwar planners followed the early planners' prescriptions by separating land uses and designing freeways to accommodate projected traffic, but these things made the cities' problems worse. Their separation of land uses generated so much traffic that all the transportation planning they did could not keep up with it. Their automobile-centered transportation planning made older neighborhoods less livable and made new neighborhoods completely unwalkable.

Today, most city planners believe that we should go back to the older model of traditional neighborhood design. We should build walkable neighborhoods with old-fashioned street grids and mixed uses that are centered on transit corridors and nodes, instead of building the single-use, freeway-oriented developments that the early planners favored. The New Urbanists have built many successful neo-traditional neighborhoods, and the smart growth movement has had some success in promoting transit-oriented development.

Yet the city planners believe that we need more top-down planning to build this sort of traditional urban development. To build old-fashioned, walkable neighborhoods, we need urban designers who control the types and locations of buildings. To build transit-oriented development, we need comprehensive regional transportation and land use planning to locate development around transit stops.

We can see the paradox most clearly in Celebration, Florida, which was built by Disney corporation and comprehensively designed by the planners to look like American towns did a century ago – before anyone had ever heard of immense corporate developers or of city planners.

According to the conventional wisdom, we need master planning today to create the sort of cities that were built without planning a century ago. Because development is large-scale and almost everyone has an automobile, developers can build massive single-use neighborhoods or build massive shopping centers outside of town that can take all the business away from Main Street. We need strict master planning to prevent this destructive style of development.

Reducing the Need for Planning

Yet in recent decades, many of our greatest successes in urban design have been the result of political action, not of planning. The anti-freeway movement of the 1960s and 1970s stopped plans to slice up the centers of American cities with freeways. The anti-sprawl movement of recent decades has stopped many proposed suburban subdivisions and shopping centers. Both of these were political movements – and citizen-activists had to spend much of their time working against projects that city planners had proposed or approved.

This book talks about taking these movements one step further: direct political limits on urban growth are the one key factor in building livable cities that our technocratic bias has made us overlook. The anti-freeway movement and the anti-sprawl movement just worked to stop destructive developments. But if we think about putting broader political limits on transportation and on the scale of development, we can begin to undo the damage that modernization has done to our cities.

This book begins by looking at the history of technocratic city planning, its utopian theories and its practical failures. Then it uses a thought experiment to show that these planners were wrong to think of cities as bundles of technical problems to be solved by experts. It looks at three possible political limitations on transportation, in combination with several possible political limitations on the scale of new development, and it shows that these different political limits on urban growth would produce cities with different ways of life. This choice of how we live is not a technical problem to be solved by planners: it is a human issue that should be a matter of personal and political choice.

These direct political limits on urban growth would not eliminate the need for planning, but they would cut the problems that the planners must deal with down to a manageable size, they would reduce the need for planning, and they would allow more individual choice and more local decision making.

Only one thing stands in the way. People are not willing to subordinate growth to political choice because they believe that our cities' problems are complex technical issues that we must leave to the planners.

Chapter 2
Completely Planned

The ideal of the planned city was invented at a time of technological optimism when people had boundless faith in modernization and growth. The early planners believed that large-scale development was an inevitable result of modern technology, and they wanted to accommodate modernization. They promoted single-function land use planning and automobile-centered transportation planning because they believed that these things were not only inevitable but would also improve people's lives. But these "inevitable" trends turned out to be less benevolent than the early planners had expected.

Functionalism and Technocracy

Though there were some earlier cases where cities were planned, city planning did not become an independent profession with its own methodology until the twentieth century. For example, Pierre Charles L'Enfant laid out Washington, DC, during the eighteenth century, but he was an architect and engineer by profession. Frederick Law Olmsted designed park and parkway systems that shaped the growth of New York and other cities during the late nineteenth century, but he was a landscape architect. Daniel Burnham designed large-scale, monumental plans for San Francisco, Chicago, and Manila, and his Beaux-Arts design for the Chicago World's Fair of 1893 inspired the early planners to build "projects," with a single land use in a specially designed area. Later city planners often quoted Burnham's famous dictum "Make no little plans,"[1] when they built civic centers and other large single-use projects, but Burnham himself was an architect and not a professional city planner.

Technological Determinism

City planning became a distinct profession during the early to mid twentieth century, when architectural theory was dominated by the functionalist school. As much as they differed on other issues, all the early city planners were influenced by functionalism.

The functionalists wanted to strip architecture of "arbitrary" ornamentation and to design buildings that were pure expressions of their materials, structures and programs. This school's dogma, "form follows function,"[2] was deterministic in its extreme interpretation: it meant that there is one technically best solution to any design problem. As one architecture critic said, "Form was merely the result of a logical process by which the operational needs and the operational techniques were brought together."[3] Because they believed that form should be determined by function, the greatest compliment that functionalists could pay a design was to call it an "honest expression" of modern materials and functions.

This sort of technological determinism was common during the early twentieth century. Jacques Ellul summed up the thinking of the functionalists and of many other modernists when he claimed that technology can determine, rationally and quantitatively, the "one best way" to manufacture a product, design a transportation system, or do any other work of modern society. The engineers can do the calculations and show you the numbers proving that their way of doing it is best. Therefore choosing a different way to do these things is no more possible than "personal choice, in respect to magnitude, between 3 and 4."[4] Even Ellul, a critic of technology, believed there was no way to avoid technological decision making in modern societies.

Technocracy

The functionalists were influenced by Thorstein Veblen's ideal of technocracy. During the early decades of the twentieth century,

Veblen argued that technological progress inevitably led to centralization and rationalization of production, which made capitalists more dependent on the production engineers. Ultimately, the economy would move beyond capitalism and production would be fully rationalized, with the entire economy under state ownership and "unreserved control by the engineers, who alone are competent to manage it."[5]

According to Veblen, the objective standards dictated by machine technology would inevitably overthrow private property and other archaic forms of authority. There would no longer be domination of one person by another when personal authority was replaced by objective technological planning: "Coercion, personal dominion, self-abasement, subjection, loyalty ... – these things do not articulate with the mechanistic conception ... the cultural drift toward the matter-of-fact...."[6]

Veblen's vision grew out of nineteenth-century socialism, which opposed traditional forms of authority and identified with industrial progress. It is obvious how much his ideas owe to Marx, who believed that modernization would inevitably lead to the overthrow of private property in favor of a centrally planned economy, where the state and other forms of authority wither away as the "domination of men" is replaced by the "administration of things." A more immediate forerunner of Veblen was the American socialist Edward Bellamy, whose book *Looking Backward* tells the story of a wealthy Bostonian who sleeps from 1887 to the year 2000 and awakens in a society that had already taken the final step of technological progress – a society where all industry is organized as a single, government-owned trust, all distribution is organized as a single department store with branches in every neighborhood, and all workers are drafted into in an "industrial army"[7] directed by the state. This book was so popular that Bellamy clubs sprang up all over America toward the end of the nineteenth century.

These earlier progressives believed that planning would be subject to some sort of humanistic direction. Marx spoke vaguely throughout his writing about the "agreed upon social plan" of the "associated producers," and Bellamy imagined that a paternalistic top management would be in control.

Veblen brought the theory into the twentieth century by removing any humanist direction of planning. He said that industry should be directed by a "Soviet of Technicians,"[8] which would plan production following the objective standards dictated by the machine itself. The entire economy should be "organized as a systematic whole, and ... managed by competent technicians with an eye single to maximum production of goods and services...."[9]

Veblen talked about the "revolutionary posture of the present state of the industrial arts."[10] Traditional societies would be swept away by purely rational planning based on the objective demands of technology.

The functionalists considered modern architects to be revolutionaries like Veblen's production engineers: they would sweep away traditional architectural forms in favor of the purely rational forms dictated by modern technology. Ludwig Mies van der Rohe first constructed the building that became an emblem of this school: his Lake Shore Drive Apartments in Chicago (1949-1951) were box-like towers with exposed steel skeletons and glass-curtain walls. The design was a pure expression of modern technology – steel and glass – in the service of a modern function – mass housing.

International Style Planning

The functionalists believed that cities, as well as individual buildings, should be designed as pure expressions of modern technology – completely planned cities. The international style was the extreme school of functionalism and it produced extreme examples of the ideal modernist city.

Le Corbusier

Le Corbusier produced the international style's most striking images of the completely planned city. His first utopia was called the "Radiant City," a planned city of three million people. In the exact center of the city, two superhighways intersected at right angles. Twenty-four identical glass-and-steel office buildings, each sixty stories high, were arranged symmetrically around the highways' intersection to form the city's business center. Residential neighborhoods surrounded the business center, with high-rise housing standing in the midst of park-like open space. Beyond this residential zone were massive factories, outside of the city proper and scattered among parks and agricultural land. Residential neighborhoods would have the high population density of about four hundred people per acre, but the apartment buildings would be tall enough that they would cover only 11% of their sites and would be surrounded by greenery. The entire city was designed as a park, residents would have open space and playing fields right at their front doors, and each apartment would have sunshine,[11] fresh air and a good view.

Another famous example of Le Corbusier's vision of the city was his Voisin Plan for Paris, which would have demolished that city's center and replaced it with a group of eighteen skyscrapers, arranged symmetrically around a superhighway. Le Corbusier developed many other proposals for housing projects that involved demolishing whole neighborhoods and replacing them with high-rise apartment buildings in a park-like setting, and this method of urban renewal was recommended by the Congres International d'Architecture Moderne in 1928.

Many of Le Corbusier's ideas were typical of modernist city planning, including his belief in the city in a park, and his belief in demolishing and replacing whole neighborhoods. He believed in standardization so strongly that, in some of his projects, he equipped all of the apartments with interchangeable mass-produced furniture, saying that "all men have the same organism, the same functions. All men have the same needs."[12]

Gropius, Breuer, and Mies

Le Corbusier's Radiant City was striking because it was a utopian design for an entire city, but it was not a perfect example of functionalism. Its symmetrical layout shows a residual Beaux-Arts influence, an "arbitrary," monumental classicism.

For an even purer functionalist vision of the city, we can turn to a plan for housing introduced in 1924 by Walter Gropius and Marcel Breuer. They proposed placing twelve-story apartment slabs at right angles to the main road and parallel to each other, with landscaped areas in between, a plan commonly used in urban housing projects during the mid twentieth century.

Gropius did studies of shadow lines to determine the optimum spacing to these buildings on objective grounds.[13] He hoped these studies would be part of a larger attempt to develop comprehensive standards for dwellings based on "the evolutionary development of man's biological and sociological life processes...."[14] Using such standards and the most efficient building materials and techniques, an architect could generate an objectively correct design for housing.

In later years, when similar housing projects by Mies van der Rohe were accused of ignoring the special "social needs" of various groups, Mies gave the typical modernist answer: "Needs are the same for everyone. Everyone wears the same clothes and drives the same kind of car. Architecture must come up not with social housing but with the right housing,"[15] and again, "Architecture is impersonal. If it isn't, it is arbitrary, as it often is. I don't want five cent social architecture, but a responsible architecture that is valid for everyone."[16]

Though Gropius and Mies did not design whole cities, their designs for housing, college campuses, industrial parks and the like added up to a modernist urban ideal.

Giedion

One of the most influential advocates of this ideal in America was Sigfried Giedion, head of the Harvard University architecture department and mentor of the postwar generation of American architects and city planners, who said that the city must be rebuilt on the "great scale" of modern technology. Parkways for cars were the first modern feature to appear in the city, and Giedion believed that "the use of a new and larger scale in town planning which would coincide with the scale already being used in the parkway system is an imperative necessity for the salvation of the city."[17]

For example, Giedion admired the Amsterdam Extension Plan of 1934, which mandated that the city's projected population growth of 250,000 people be accommodated in a series of public housing projects of 10,000 dwelling units each. The new scale of development allowed the project to be designed by experts in housing, and it required planning, particularly demographic projection, to insure that the housing built would meet the demand that existed when each project was completed. Giedion noted with admiration that Amsterdam's plan "is based on careful consideration of all those factors which determine the social make-up of a community. All measures proposed have their foundation in the figures that come under the heading of vital statistics – birth and death rates, immigration and emigration totals, etc."[18]

Giedion also admired New York's Rockefeller Center as an example of the "great scale" of modern technology because it is a unified design for a cluster of office buildings in an area much larger than a traditional city block. Giedion's only reservation about Rockefeller Center was that it was surrounded by "the chaos of midtown Manhattan"[19] – in other words, that it was integrated with the surrounding city streets, rather than being surrounded and defined by parks and parkways. Large unified designs like this must be clearly separated from other land uses, he said, to avoid the traditional city's "chaotic intermingling of functions."[20]

The International Style Vision

Remarkable as it may seem today, Giedion and his contemporaries took the name "parkway" seriously, and they believed that freeways would serve as the spines of our cities' park systems. Giedion also admired the parkways themselves as esthetic objects: their "bridges, their mounting drives and the modern sculpture of numberless single and triple cloverleaves prove that the possibilities of a great scale are inherent in our period."[21]

In keeping with this "great scale," the arrangement known as the "superblock" was the primary unit of modern planning. Civic centers, industrial parks, office parks, housing projects, and centers for the performing arts were all supposed to be built in areas much larger than a traditional city block so each could be designed as a unified whole by experts in its function. Automobile traffic would be rationalized on parkways and arterial streets, which would surround the city's superblocks and define them as separate. Streets and walkways within the superblock would be designed only for local access; the parkways and arterial streets would carry all through traffic.

Separating land uses in this way would let each serve its purpose more efficiently. For example, in older cities, through traffic used residential and business streets: the cars made the streets less safe and less pleasant for people who lived and worked there, and the people slowed down traffic when they crossed the street or parked their cars on the street. The city would function much more efficiently if there were separate superblocks for housing and for business, separate off-street parking, and separate freeways and arterial streets for through traffic. Then residents and workers would not be disturbed by traffic, and traffic would not be slowed down by pedestrians or by drivers stopping to parallel park.

Separating uses also made it possible for the superblocks and roads to be designed by experts. Just as industrial engineers could design modern factories that were more efficient than the small workshops of the past, planners could design freeways that carried traffic more efficiently than the urban streets of the past, and design housing projects, business districts, civic centers, and recreation areas that performed their specialized functions more efficiently than the mixed-use urban neighborhoods of the past.

All of these efficiently designed land uses and transportation corridors would be coordinated by the master plan. The master plan would locate the individual land uses in appropriate places, and would ensure that the city had the housing, transportation, recreation, and other services that it needed to accommodate its economic development and population growth.

As extreme functionalists, these planners believed that there was one correct design for the modern city, dictated by modern technology; the beauty of the city lay in the "honesty" and clarity of its expression of this technological design. Buildings were abstract sculptures expressing their functions, and they could be appreciated as esthetic objects because they stood in park-like open space. The city as a whole, with its superblocks and transportation corridors, had the clarity of a flowchart.

The functionalists' ideal was based on their belief that the modern, technological economy required housing, industrial production, transportation, recreation, and so on, to be provided by centralized organizations geared up for large-scale production. This completely centralized economy required completely planned cities.

Garden City and Regional Planning

Despite their technological optimism, the international style planners designed cities to defend people against the damaging side effects of technology. Le Corbusier located the factories of his Radiant City on its outskirts, surrounded by open space, in order to protect residents from the industrial pollution that was typical of nineteenth century factory cities. These planners also separated through traffic on arterial routes to defend housing and business districts from high-speed traffic.

A second school of early city planners – called the garden city planners or the regionalists – shared this faith in functional rationalization, but it put more emphasis on defending people from the side-effects of technology than the international style planners.

Howard and the Garden City

The garden city was invented by Ebenezer Howard, an English court reporter whose avocation was city planning. Howard read Bellamy's *Looking Backward* in 1888, the year of its publication, and finished it in a single sitting; the next morning, he said, "I went into some of the crowded parts of London, and as I passed through the narrow dark streets ... and reflected on the absolute unsoundness of our economic system, there came to me an overpowering sense of the temporary nature of all I saw, and of its entire unsuitability for ... the new order...."[22] He was associated with the Radicals, non-Marxist progressives who believed in peaceful evolution toward a collective society.

In 1898, Howard published his blueprint for rebuilding cities, *To-morrow: A Peaceful Path to Real Reform*, which was reissued in 1902 under the title *Garden Cities of Tomorrow*.[23] Howard wanted to break up the large cities of his time and disperse workers into planned Garden Cities of about 30,000 people each. He diagrammed the Garden City as a series of concentric circles. In the center was a park with civic buildings such as a town hall, library, museum, and hospital. Around this was a shopping arcade in a "crystal palace," which would also be used as a winter garden. Then came two rings of relatively low-density residences with private gardens, separated from each other by Grand Avenue, a broad boulevard planted with trees and greenery. The residential rings were divided into neighborhoods of 5,000 people, each with a school and church in its center. The Garden City would occupy 1,000 acres in the middle of a 5,000 acre agricultural and forest preserve, which would act as a greenbelt to separate it from other cities. Factories would be located in this greenbelt, separated from residences. Howard hoped that these Garden Cities would lure most workers out of London and other large cities, so their slums could be demolished and turned into parks.

In 1899, Howard formed the Garden City Association, which built two garden cities, Letchworth (1903) and Welwyn (1920). Letchworth, designed by Raymond Unwin was based on Howard's model. Welwyn included only housing and had an average density of only 5 units per acre – a large step toward modern suburbia. Later Garden City planners led the fight for zoning laws to segregate housing from other functions and to restrict densities to low, suburban levels.

The Garden City was meant to protect workers from the side-effects of modern technology by lowering densities and separating residents from factories. Yet Howard was inspired by Bellamy's technological optimism, and he believed that workers would be protected when modernization brought us something like Bellamy's vision of a completely planned society.

Geddes and Regional Planning

Howard's original Garden City was meant to reduce the need for traveling by combining work, residence, shopping, and recreation in one town. Patrick Geddes extended this principle of reducing the need for transportation to the entire region. His idea of regional planning was popularized by his most influential disciple, Lewis Mumford.

Geddes, Mumford, and other regionalists believed that entire economic regions should be planned as integral units, so they could be relatively self-sufficient economically. Regional planners should locate a region's factories, homes, and cities in a way that minimizes the transportation of people, raw materials, and finished goods. Decentralizing the national economy into a number of regional economies would also make cities smaller: for example, New York had grown so large because it was a financial center of the national and world economy, and so Mumford claimed that "to diminish the traffic at Times Square it may be necessary to reroute the export of wheat from the hinterland...."[24]

Regionalists insisted on local production because they were repelled by the international style planners' idea that modern technology required the same architecture world-wide. They hoped distinct regional styles would develop, based on each area's natural resources, climate, and geography.

Yet the regionalists attacked the international style in the name of rational technocratic planning. For example, they believed that we had national production and inefficient "cross-hauling" of goods only because the national economy was dominated by moneyed interests, and regional production would take over when there were rationally planned international, national and regional economies. For example, New York state used to be a major grain producer; grain from the Midwest took over the national market because of the influence of the major flour companies; New York would become self-sufficient in grain again when the entire North American economy and world economy were rationally planned to eliminate this unnecessary transportation of grain and flour.

The regionalists wanted to replace political divisions, such as state and city governments, with the functional divisions used for regional, continental, or global planning. For example, Mumford said the nation state is obsolete because it "is usually too big to define a single region, with its political, economic and social elements in symmetrical relationships, and it is too small to include a whole society, like that of Western Europe or the North American continent, which must ultimately become the sphere of a larger system of cooperative administration."[25]

The sort of planning used in the most modern sectors of the economy should be extended to all of society; as Mumford said: "Plan and order are latent in all modern industrial processes. ... What is still lacking is the transference of these techniques from industry to the social order at large."[26] The planners would control every aspect of life; as Mumford said, "To achieve all these possible gains in production ... requires the services of the geographer and regional planner, the psychologist, the educator, the sociologist.... Perhaps

Russia alone at present has the necessary framework for this planning in its fundamental institutions; but to one degree or another ... other countries are moving in the same direction...."[27]

Geddes and Mumford rewrote the conventional modernist history of the "inevitable" effects of the machine on civilization. The international style planners believed in the conventional idea that modernization meant larger scale production, more centralization, and larger cities. The regionalists said that things were more complicated: in the nineteenth century, large-scale, centralizing "paleotechnic" methods of production had replaced handicraft production, but in the twentieth century these older methods would be replaced by decentralizing "neotechnic" methods of production. For example, steam power had concentrated workers around a single source of energy during the nineteenth century, but it was being replaced by electrical power, which creates a grid of energy dispersed through a whole region. The railroad concentrated population around a single main line during the nineteenth century, but it was being replaced by the automobile, which makes the entire region accessible. The regionalists were technological determinists, like the international style planners, but they believed that twentieth-century technologies would inevitably disperse population and lower densities, rather than concentrating population in large, dense cities.

Common Ideas of Early Planners

The regionalists often attacked the international style for being massive and impersonal, but we can see in retrospect that the two schools had many ideas in common.

Like the international style planners, the regionalists believed in separating land uses so each could be designed by experts in its function. Mumford argued throughout his career that separating arterial and residential streets would improve both the quality of the neighborhood and the flow of traffic by providing each with specialized facilities. Likewise, he captions one of the photographs in *The Culture of Cities*: "Modern industrial plant: lifted out from the entangling street land: a well designed zone appropriately designed for its special needs. Discontinuous zoning of quarters ... is characteristic of the New Urban plan: each function placed in a specially designed environment and deliberately separated from the flow of traffic except for access."[28] As a functionalist, Mumford also believed this separation of functions had esthetic value: he captions another photograph, of a monotonous housing tract, a small belt of farmland, and a massive factory complex: "the separation of the industrial zone, the agricultural zone and the domestic zone is admirably clarified."[29]

Like the international style planners, the regionalists believed that these separate land uses should be surrounded and defined by the freeways and arterial streets that carried through traffic, and that their internal streets should be used only for local access. Mumford's associates, Henry Wright and Clarence Stein, invented what has become conventional suburban street design in their plan for Radburn, New Jersey, located in the midst of farmland between New York City and Philadelphia. Houses were arranged in superblocks, which were surrounded by arterial streets and were accessible via cul-de-sacs; there were also pedestrian walkways to the houses, separated from the streets. Mumford commented, "Here was the first town built anywhere that consistently abandoned the corridor avenue lined with houses, that divorced the functions of living from the noise and traffic of the street, and that provided a continuous belt of park space within the residential superblocks...."[30] In the original plan, Radburn's housing was meant to be part of a functionally balanced Garden City; but financing disappeared before the rest was built, so residents had to commute to New York or Philadelphia for work.

Like the international style planners, the regionalists considered the automobile the inevitable form of transportation in the modern city, and they had great hopes for the automobile because they believed (correctly) that it would reduce density. They claimed that a member of their school invented the freeway: Benton MacKaye had come up with an early proposal for what he called "townless highways," free of shopping and other unrestricted access, which he claimed would bring "highwayless towns" as their necessary corollary.[31] Even Lewis Mumford, who was influential as a critic of the automobile in later years, claimed enthusiastically during the technologically optimistic 1930s that "The motor car has decentralized transportation radically."[32]

Like the international style planners, the regionalists believed in demolishing old neighborhoods and replacing them with modern housing. Le Corbusier wanted to demolish central Paris and replace it with towers in a park. Ebenezer Howard wanted to demolish the slums of the old cities and replace them with tracts of housing in the countryside. Henry Wright argued that older homes were so much less efficiently designed than modern housing that "even though they may not be dilapidated..., they might be torn down with at most a very small loss in terms of money."[33]

Like the international style planners, the regionalists believed that each separate land use would be designed by planners who were experts in its function, and that the work of these specialists would be coordinated by master planning. If anything, they were more impressed by the idea of master planning than the international style planners were. For example, Mumford said, "Regional planning is the conscious direction and collective integration of all those activities which rest upon the use of the earth.... Hence, regional planning is a further stage in the more specialized or isolated processes of agriculture planning, industry planning, or city planning."[78]

Like the international style planners, the regionalists believed in functionalist architecture and in technological determinism. For example, Mumford became known as a critic of impersonal, standardized housing during the postwar period, but in his 1930s book *Technics and Civilization*, which was strongly influenced by Veblen's technocracy and by functionalism, he includes an illustration of "modern workers' dwellings in Sweden" that looks like a typical mobile-home development, identical little boxes lined up in perfectly straight rows, which he describes as "the sudden crystallization of neotechnic methods in community planning and housing ... a handsome and well integrated human environment."[34]

Likewise, during the postwar period, Mumford insisted that technology must be subordinated to moral control – in large part, because he was shaken by the use of the atomic bomb[35] – but during the 1930s, he reduced all human questions to technical problems that can be solved by the life sciences, which he takes to include psychology and sociology as well as biology. He believed that these sciences would inevitably lead us to an economy scientifically planned around our biological needs. The next step beyond "neotechnic planning" would be what he named "biotechnic planning."[36]

Technocratic thinking seemed so compelling during the 1930's that even the most sensitive American critic of technology could not escape from it. During the postwar years, Mumford would change his views and admit that technological organizations could stifle people's freedom – though this new idea did not make him question his older ideal of the completely planned city – but during the 1930s, Mumford believed that technology could be abused only if it is controlled by private property, the state and other traditional forms of power. Abuses would all be eliminated when these arbitrary forms of power were replaced with purely objective planning.

Project and Accommodate

The international style planners and the regionalists differed about the proper density and scale of modern cities, but as we have seen, they agreed on many fundamental principles of urban design.

The early planners all agreed that city's land uses should be separated into single-function zones or superblocks, much larger than a conventional city block. The interiors of these zones should be park-like, with free-standing buildings surrounded by open space, rather than rows of buildings facing streets. Their internal circulation systems should be designed for local access only, and larger arterial streets and parkways that surrounded them should carry all the through traffic. These single-function zones and the transportation routes should each be designed by experts in its function – industrial planners, housers, traffic engineers, and so on – and the work of all these specialist planners should be coordinated by master planning. Thus, the city's design was controlled by technical decisions that the planners make, not by political decisions that citizens make. This completely planned city was the inevitable result of economic modernization.

Practical planners, even in the 1930s, tended to focus on these common features of the planned city and to ignore the debates between the international style planners and the regionalists about density and scale. For example, Clarence Perry, a practical houser, developed the very influential "neighborhood unit formula" in his 1939 book, *Housing for the Machine Age*. He said that a neighborhood unit should be built as a superblock with an elementary school in the center. Its internal street system should be "designed to facilitate circulation within the unit and to discourage its use by through traffic," and "the unit should be bounded on all sides by arterial streets, sufficiently wide to facilitate its by-passing … by through traffic."[37] These wide arterial streets would also define the neighborhood visually.[38] Within the unit, there would be housing in a park-like setting, and shopping would be restricted to the arterial streets. Perry adopted the ideal of building park-like superblocks surrounded by wide arterial streets, which was common to the international style planners and the regionalists, and he ignored their disputes about density: he recommended a continuum of increasing densities, from suburbs to high-rises, as you moved from the outskirts to the center of the city.[39]

The Chicago School of Planners

In postwar America, the ideological differences between the international style planners and the regionalists evaporated in the face of a "value-free" methodology which grew out of the work of a third school of planners that is not as well known as the first two, the Chicago School of Planners.

These urban sociologists – the most important of whom were Robert Park, Louis Wirth, and Robert Redfield – developed a new method of analyzing the city's growth, which they called "human ecology." To project the future growth of cities, they used a model based on the distribution of species in an ecological community in nature; the city's functions were interrelated and, when one was altered, the entire pattern would change. Borrowing terms from natural ecologists, Park spoke of new functions or populations "invading" an area of a city, and he called the patterned change that follows "succession." Park claimed that the city "has a more or less typical order and pattern in the territorial distribution of its component unity. Furthermore, as numbers increase, this pattern is likely to exhibit a typical succession of changes."[40] Thus, "Studies of succession ... seek ... to make change intelligible, so that it can eventually be controlled by technical devices or political measures."[41] Wirth explained that "the ecological aspect of human life yields a degree of objective knowledge, in the sense of noncontroversial description of physical facts[,] and offers possibilities for a high degree of mensuration and precision."[42]

Park's 1915 essay, "The City: Suggestions for the Investigation of Human Behavior in the City Environment,"[43] stimulated a flurry of empirical research. When he rewrote this essay in 1952, Park added a description of how widely his method had spread:

The Bell Telephone Company is now making, particularly in New York and Chicago, elaborate investigations, the purpose of which is to determine, in advance of its actual changes, the probable growth and distribution of the urban population within the metropolitan areas. The Sage Foundation ... sought to find mathematical formulae that would enable them to predict future expansion and limits of population in New York City. The recent development of chain stores has made the problem of location a matter of concern to different chain store corporations. The result has been the rise of a new profession. There is now a class of experts whose sole occupation is to ... locate, with something like scientific accuracy, ... restaurants, cigar stores, drug stores, and other smaller retail business units...."[44]

Of course, the complex mathematical methods used to plan cities are beyond the grasp of ordinary people. Park believed that it was no longer appropriate to choose city officials through democratic elections because "the problems of city government have become, with the growth and organization of city life, so complicated that it is no longer desirable to leave them to the control of men whose only qualification ... [is] that they have succeeded in gaining office...."[45] Park distrusted what he called "the mob," and he hoped that research in "collective psychology" would develop new psychological techniques that could be used in combination with economic techniques to "exercise a useful control over the trend of prices and events."[46]

The End of Ideology

Appeals to objective, value-free techniques of planning and projecting future trends had a great deal of weight in postwar America.

At the time, sociologists were saying that America had reached "the end of ideology," that the old political disputes were being replaced by the pragmatic use of technology to solve problems.[47] Likewise, John F. Kennedy said:

> Most of us are conditioned for many years to have a political viewpoint – Republican or Democratic, liberal, conservative or moderate. The fact of the matter is that most of the problems … that we now face are technical problems, are administrative problems. They are very sophisticated judgments, … questions which are now beyond the comprehension of most men ….[48]

In postwar America, practical city planners generally accepted existing demographic and economic trends and tried to control projected growth so it would take the form that both the international style and the regionalist planners believed in. Practical planners used zoning and built housing projects to organize projected growth in single-use areas, and they laid out freeways and arterial streets to rationalize projected traffic.

City planning had established itself as a new profession with its own methodology during the early to mid twentieth century, as Park said. The field is named "city planning" because of its early technocratic bias. At the time, people believed the only way to make cities more livable was through planning.

Chapter 3
Postwar American Planning

Modernist city planning was considered radical and avant garde during the 1920s and 1930s, but it became standard practice in postwar America. The avant garde claimed that it was leading society into the future, and it was right: the modernist vision dominated city planning in postwar America precisely because it fit the scale of modern technology, just as the planners had claimed. The nineteenth-century city was laid out with a grid of streets for the convenience of small developers who bought street frontage by the foot; the postwar modern city was laid out in superblocks and zones for the convenience of the big developers who build business parks, shopping centers, and tract housing. This is the "great scale" of modern technology.

The conventional wisdom is that our cities' problems are caused by lack of planning, but in reality, many of our cities' problems are the direct result of postwar planning that followed the ideals of the early planners. In postwar America, city planners accepted the modernist ideal of a completely planned city, and they used it as the basis of their planning to provide transportation, to provide housing, to redevelop slums, and to make our cities more orderly by separating functions. And now it is widely recognized that they made our cities' problems worse.

Planning for Congestion

According to the conventional wisdom, our cities are congested and automobile dependent because of lack of planning. In reality, these problems are worse because traffic engineers and other planners in postwar America followed the prescriptions that the early planning theorists had laid out during the first half of the twentieth century.

The early planners said that we could solve our transportation problems by projecting future traffic volume and building enough freeways and high-speed arterial streets to accommodate it. Because these roads were specially designed for transportation and free from other uses, the traffic would flow more efficiently. They would not have the congestion that you find in older cities, where streets are multipurpose, so through traffic is constantly interrupted by pedestrians crossing and cars stopping to park.

Government planners implemented this vision in postwar America. Federal transportation planning began under the Roosevelt Administration, which funded highways to provide construction jobs for the unemployed. During the postwar period, Federal funding expanded dramatically: the Eisenhower administration began planning and building the 41,000 mile Interstate Highway System, which dominates American transportation today, and created the Highway Trust Fund to provide an endlessly expanding source of funding for these highways by guaranteeing that revenues from gasoline taxes would be used only for highway spending.[49] During the postwar period, traffic engineers also laid out the new suburbs with wide arterial streets with no on-street parking to speed traffic. This large scale of development required planning: traffic engineers projected future traffic volumes, and they provided the freeway and street capacity to accommodate this traffic.

Yet with all this planning, traffic kept getting worse. The projections of traffic volumes on urban freeways always turned out to be underestimates. Freeways that were supposed to accommodate traffic for a decade became congested within a year or two of being completed.

Induced Demand

Today, city planners call this problem "induced demand." Building freeways allows people to travel faster, and so it encourages people to travel longer distances. In the short term, higher speeds encourage people to drive to regional shopping centers rather than to local shopping. In the longer term, higher speeds encourage people to move to low density suburbs and commute longer distances to work.

One study found that, within five years after a major freeway is built in California, 95% of the new road capacity fills up with traffic that would not have existed if the road had not been built.[50] In Great Britain, transportation planners are no longer allowed to count reduced travel time as a benefit of building a new freeway: the Department of Transport has adopted a guidance document saying that cost-benefit studies on new freeways must assume that elasticity of demand may be as high as 1.0 with respect to speed – which means that average trip length increases as much as speed increases, so higher speeds just lengthen trips and do not save any time.[51]

Postwar planners rationalized traffic on freeways and arterial streets, but this did not eliminate traffic congestion and protect people from cars, as the early planners had expected. Instead, these high-speed roads generated more traffic, dramatically increasing automobile use and the problems it causes.

The costs of the automobile are now immense. A century ago, when income was much lower, Americans spent only 1% or 2% of their income on transportation. Today, as Jerome Segal says, the average American family works from January 1 until March 14 just to pay for transportation: "No society in history has worked so much just to be able to get around."[52]

Subsidies to the Automobile

There are also immense public subsidies to the automobile. Though many people believe the automobile pays for itself because gasoline taxes finance highway construction, the fact is that historically, only about 60% of spending on roads is paid for by gasoline taxes, and the rest of the funding comes from general taxes, property taxes, and sales taxes used to fund local roads.[53] For example, in the state of New Jersey, drivers pay only $2.5 billion a year in taxes and user fees, while the state spends $3.2 billion a year on roads.[54] In addition, cities' general funds pay for local streets and for policing and traffic lights.

The automobile also has huge environmental costs. It is the number one cause of urban noise and air pollution, and one of the major causes of global warming. And automobiles have killed over 3,200,000 Americans, more than twice as many as the total number of Americans who died in all the wars the country has fought in its history.

Automobiles also take up huge amounts of valuable urban land. It takes eight lanes of street to carry the same number of people by car that a single lane could accommodate if they rode in buses or trolley cars,[55] and it takes eight lanes of freeway to carry the number of people that could travel on one track of commuter rail.[56] A parking space for a single automobile takes up a bit more space than the floor space per worker in a modern office building: the rule of thumb is 250 to 300 square feet of land for a parking space (including the driving lanes and landscaping of the parking lot) versus 250 square feet of floor space per office worker.

Planning for Sprawl

According to the conventional wisdom, our cities also suffer from suburban sprawl because of lack of planning. In reality, the major causes of sprawl in postwar America were the federal and state freeway planners who made long-distance commutes possible, and federal housing planners and local zoning boards who encouraged suburbanization.

As we have seen, the garden city planners said that we should use zoning to hold down densities, that we should separate housing from other functions, and that we should design housing tracts which are surrounded by wide arterial streets for through traffic and which have internal street systems used only for local access.

Federal Housing Policy and Local Zoning

The federal government began to promote sprawl actively during the 1930s. The New Deal's Greenbelt Town Program was inspired and administered by Rexford Tugwell, who wanted to build communities based on the theories of Ebenezer Howard. As Tugwell said, "My idea is to go just outside of centers of population, pick up cheap land, build a whole community and entice people into it. Then go back into the cities and tear down whole slums and make parks of them."[57] But this program was criticized by conservatives and succeeded in building only three garden cities.

The federal government's programs to insure new suburban mortgages were much more successful.

The Home Owner's Loan Corporation (HOLC), created in 1933 to provide loans to home owners who were in danger of defaulting, was the first of these programs. This agency invented the long-term self-amortizing mortgage. During the 1920s, mortgages typically lasted for five to ten years and did not pay off the full cost of the house, so they had to be renewed when they expired. The HOLC was created to help people who were in danger of losing their homes because the depression made it impossible for them to renew their mortgages. To make sure these long-term mortgages were secure, the HOLC did extensive planning (as we will see) and biased its loans toward suburban neighborhoods.[58]

The Federal Housing Authority was established in 1934 to insure mortgages for newly purchased homes. Until the 1960s, it followed the lead of the HOLC and offered financing only to new construction at suburban densities.

FHA standards were reinforced by local planning. In the new suburbs, the local zoning laws required low densities, allowed only housing within residential neighborhoods, and restricted shopping to the arterial streets. The traffic engineers built wide arterial streets around neighborhoods of winding streets and cul-de-sacs. The typical suburban landscape of low density housing and strip malls is often criticized as a "disorderly" result of unplanned development, but it is actually a direct result of zoning and of street design that separates local and through traffic, policies advocated by the early planners and adopted by practical planners during the postwar period.

Some of the most notorious examples of suburban sprawl followed the planners' ideas even more carefully: most of Daly City, California, which inspired the song "Little Boxes Made of Ticky-Tacky," consists of the vast subdivision of Westlake, whose design was inspired by Clarence Perry's neighborhood unit concept: as a guide to Bay Area architecture says, it has "elementary school centered, through traffic free, residential neighborhood units, an articulated park and recreational open space system, and high school facilities, just like the textbooks say it should."[59]

During the postwar period, the planners carried out their policy of promoting suburbanization with astounding effectiveness. In the single decade following 1950, for example, the number of dwelling units in the United States increased by 63%.[60] The new dwelling units built in a couple of decades after the war outnumbered all the housing that had ever been built in the country previously. In this short time, modern suburbia became the dominant form of American community, with more population than the cities or the countryside.

Suburbia and Popular Demand

We often hear that suburbia expanded so quickly only because people wanted to live there. It is true that there was pent-up demand for housing after World War II and that many people wanted to take advantage of postwar prosperity to buy their own houses. But there is no reason to think that they wanted houses in postwar suburbia, designed according to the planners' principles, rather than similar houses in neighborhoods designed like old-fashioned streetcar suburbs.

In fact, the data we have shows that most of the people who moved to the new postwar suburbs did not particularly want to live in this sort of neighborhood. When Herbert Gans interviewed the residents of Levittown, a name that was symbolic of the mass suburbs of the fifties, he found that 72% of them had moved there for reasons that had nothing to do with its suburban setting. Only about 28% gave reasons that had any connection with suburban living: "relaxed, peaceful, outdoor living," "working around the house and yard," and "privacy and freedom of action in owned home."[61] The vast majority moved to Levittown for "house related" reasons, either because their previous homes were too cramped or because Levittown provided the best house available for the money. Judging from their responses, even the minority who gave reasons for moving that were connected with suburban living would have been just as happy with a house in a neighborhood designed like an old-fashioned streetcar suburb. But streetcar suburbs were not being built at the time because they were not allowed by zoning laws.

Though Gans did not make this point (and, in fact, was interested in defending the postwar suburbs), his statistics show that the vast majority of Levittowners had never given any thought to whether they wanted to live in suburbia: they were passive consumers of housing built according to standards that the planners imposed on them.

During the prosperous postwar period, many people were able to buy their own homes for the first time, so there certainly was demand for more private houses. But there is no reason to think that people wanted to move to the land of cul-de-sacs, strip malls, and total automobile dependency. This sprawl exists not because of consumer choice but because of planning by local zoning boards and the Federal Housing Authority.

Planning for Blight

Automobile-centered planning did not just generate sprawl by letting people commute longer distances; it also generated sprawl because freeways and traffic blighted older neighborhoods. Urban neighborhoods and older suburbs of the 1920s absorbed much of the traffic generated by the new postwar suburbs. Neighborhoods that had been quiet suburbs themselves in 1900 or 1925 were flooded by traffic from the new suburbs, driving through them to the city center or driving to them for shopping.

Many new developments in the older neighborhoods, such as hospital centers, were designed as superblocks that excluded traffic from their interiors and created traffic congestion on nearby city streets

Older neighborhoods were sliced apart by freeways: people could no longer walk to the nearby shopping street after a freeway was put in their way. Their housing stock was decimated to clear land for freeway rights of way or for parking lots. For example, in New York, to build a single approach-way to one early freeway, the city condemned buildings containing over four thousand apartments.[62] In Boston, all of the highways that were planned would have displaced 5% of the city's total population.[63]

Because of all of the traffic that the new freeways generated, people living in old neighborhoods had to put up with noise, dirty air, and congestion. Streets that had once been empty enough for children to play in filled up with cars. Naturally, many residents of these neighborhoods moved out to the suburbs themselves, looking for more pleasant places to live and safer places for their children to play.

Redlining

In addition to building freeways through older neighborhoods, federal planners invented the practice of "redlining" certain neighborhoods – refusing loans to any property in the neighborhood, however good the owner's credit was. This practice became notorious after banks imitated it, but few realize that the federal planners initiated it.

We have seen that the Home Owner's Loan Corporation (HOLC) was established in 1933, and it invented the long-term, self-amortizing mortgage. To make sure that the houses would keep their value through the life of the mortgage, HOLC systematized appraisal methods throughout the nation. It divided cities into neighborhoods, developed questionnaires to gather information about the occupations, incomes and ethnicities of residents and the age, price range and state of repair of the housing stock. On the basis of this information, it drew up "Residential Security Maps" that rated the neighborhoods of every city in the country. Grade A neighborhoods were colored green on the maps and were described as new and homogeneous (meaning they had no immigrants or African Americans). Grade B neighborhoods were colored blue and were described as "still desirable" though they had "reached their peak." Grade C neighborhoods were colored yellow and were described as "definitely declining." Grade D neighborhoods were colored red and were described as neighborhoods that had already declined. Neighborhoods were invariably rated as Grade D if they had poor maintenance or vandalism or if they had a substantial African-American population. Neighborhoods with an "infiltration of Jews" were rated Grade B or lower.

This planning was based on the work of the Chicago school of planners. Homer Hoyt, who worked closely with Robert Park at the

University of Chicago, developed a model of neighborhood evolution that showed how housing values changed as the economic status of residents changed. He found that the entry of African-Americans into a neighborhood would initially raise prices (as the first families paid a premium to break the color barrier) but then lower prices dramatically, so it would mean a D rating for the neighborhood.[64]

The Federal Housing Administration (FHA) followed the lead of the HOLC. In a 1938 directive, the FHA demanded that the neighborhoods where it made loans should be evaluated for their "social characteristics," with the rating based primarily upon "the group income characteristics of the occupant group at the immediate neighborhood of a location." To make sure that the neighborhoods would remain viable for the life of the mortgage, it also required that "areas surrounding a location are investigated to determine whether incompatible racial and social groups are present, for the purpose of making a prediction regarding the probability of the location being invaded by such groups."[65] The FHA's planners were also drawing on the theories of the Chicago school, which used "invaded" as a technical term.

Based on this policy, the FHA "redlined" large areas of inner cities and refused to guarantee their mortgages. The term "redlined" apparently came from the colors used for Grade D neighborhoods in the HOLC maps.[66]

Banks were imitating the HOLC and FHA practices by the end of the 1930s. When the Federal Home Loan Bank Board sent a questionnaire asking about their lending practices, banks responded that the most desirable lending areas were "A and B" or "FHA only," and that they would not make loans to "red" or to "red and most yellow."[67]

The predictions that these neighborhoods would decline were self-fulfilling prophesies. With loan money cut off, these neighborhoods became blighted, despite the widespread prosperity of the postwar decades.

Slum Clearance

What was the solution to urban blight? Obviously, it was even more modernist planning.

Slum clearance and federal housing projects began during the 1930s, but their numbers soared during the postwar period. Title I of the Housing Act of 1949 provided federal grants and loans to local governments for slum clearance and redevelopment. The Housing Act of 1954 provided more funding for urban renewal, with an emphasis on clearing slums and replacing them with commercial developments and high-rise housing for the middle class. Then, motivated by outcries that that urban renewal displaced the poor, the Model Cities program of 1966 emphasized clearing slums to provide both services (such as education, health care, and employment) and better housing for the poor. All of these programs tore down slums and replaced them with housing projects built according to the international-style model – towers in a park designed according to government standards that prescribed proper ratios of floor space, recreational facilities, open space, and so on per resident (like the objective standards for housing that Gropius had worked to develop).

In some cases, redevelopment planners stepped in even before the bankers redlined neighborhoods and declared that they were slums that should be cleared. This was also a self-fulfilling prophecy: once a neighborhood was declared a slum, the banks stopped lending to it, so it quickly became a slum. As Jane Jacobs points out, the bankers' redlining maps and the redevelopment agencies' slum-clearance maps both came into common use at about the same time, were identical in conception and were usually identical in results.[68]

Consider the fate of East Harlem in New York, which was a stable Italian and Puerto Rican neighborhood with hundreds of voluntary organizations and thousands of small businesses, many of them run by the second or third generation of owners. In 1937, a city-sponsored study found that the neighborhood was likely to become New York's center of Italian culture. But in 1942, the banks redlined the neighborhood; they even closed all the bank branches in this neighborhood of 100,000 people, so merchants had to go to other neighborhoods to deposit their receipts. Some parts of the neighborhood held out despite the redlining, but during the 1950s the redevelopers decided to clear its slums by building the huge Wagner Houses housing project, completed in 1958, which has 2,154 apartments in 22 buildings located between First and Second Avenues and 120th to 124th Streets. In order to clear the land for this project, the planners destroyed buildings containing over 1,300 businesses and over 500 non-commercial storefront organizations. More than four-fifths of the proprietors of these businesses were ruined financially, because redevelopment did not compensate business owners for the value of their businesses as going concerns, though they did compensate property owners for the value of property they took. When they drove people out of their homes and businesses, the Housing Authority's own managers said they were amazed to see how many of them had improved their properties substantially. But the neighborhood could not survive the massive destruction of its businesses and civic associations by this project, and it became one of New York's worst slums.[69]

Even the conventional wisdom does not blame these housing projects on lack of planning, since their designs followed the ideas of the early city planning theorists very closely.

But despite the planners' theories, most projects were worse than the slums they replaced. Studies found that they had more crime than older slums with the same socio-economic conditions.[70] For example, when things were at their worst, a single housing project, the Robert Taylor Homes complex, accounted for about 10% of the crime in Chicago.[71] The impersonal functionalist design of the projects caused a breakdown of civic life: there were no eyes on the street, and people living in high-rises with long, impersonal corridors were unlikely to know their neighbors. The projects were vandalized by their own tenants, and they were shunned by anyone who had the choice. The blight spread from the projects to the adjacent neighborhoods: because the projects had no shopping, people from nearby neighborhoods had no reason to walk to them, and the decline in pedestrian traffic hurt businesses on adjacent streets.

The Pruitt-Igoe housing in St. Louis, an early project that was hailed as an example of enlightened public housing policy and given an award by the American Institute of Architects when it was designed in 1951, suffered from so much crime and vandalism that the city had to demolish parts of it twenty years later. Pruitt-Igoe's demolition started a trend. The federal department of Housing and Urban Development established the HOPE VI program in 1992 to systematically demolish the worst housing projects and replace them with mixed use developments designed like old-fashioned neighborhoods, with housing and shopping facing streets. HOPE VI has demolished over 57,000 severely distressed housing units.[72]

From Blight and Flight to Gentrification

As inner cities declined, there was a vicious circle of urban blight and suburban flight, which became a major generator of suburban sprawl during the postwar period. During the 1950s, people felt they had the choice of leaving the city and moving to the new suburbs, but by the 1960s, many people felt they were forced to flee to the suburbs, as the term "inner city" became synonymous with "slum." As the middle class moved beyond the city limits, cities lost their regions' best taxpayers to the suburbs, but they kept providing services to the poor and to the suburbanites who commuted in, and this fiscal squeeze led to cutbacks in services that made them even less livable.

Urban blight was a major concern during the 1950s and the 1960s, and there were endless demands for more federal money and more planning to deal with it, though this blight was largely the result of planning, as we have seen: blight began to spread through our cities because of the federal money spent on urban freeways and the FHA's decision to fund only mortgages in new suburbs. And federal money for slum clearance and housing projects only made the problem worse.

Redlining was illegalized by the Housing Act of 1961. During the 1960s, the federal government virtually stopped building urban freeways because of local opposition. During the 1970s, the federal government virtually stopped building housing projects because conservative administrations cut funding for them. Though federal housing policy still discriminates against urban neighborhoods,[73] cities began spontaneously improving after the most destructive planning ended. By the 1980s, people stopped talking about the crisis of urban "blight and flight", and instead "gentrification" became the new byword as the middle class began to move back to the cities.

Some of our most successfully gentrified urban neighborhoods would not exist if the planners had had their way. In New York, for example, Robert Moses planned to demolish West Greenwich Village and to replace its winding streets of tenements and row-houses with superblocks of tower-in-a-park housing. He also planned to demolish a swath of the neighborhood now called SOHO to clear the right-of-way for the Lower-Manhattan Expressway, one of three freeways he planned to cut across Manhattan. Since then, both of these area have improved spontaneously and turned into two of New York city's most desirable neighborhoods, but they would have been destroyed if citizens had not mobilized politically to stop the planners.

Planning Functionally

The freeways, suburbs, and urban housing projects all followed the cardinal rule of modernist urban planning: a city's land uses should be separated so each can be designed by experts to perform its function most effectively. Because freeways were separated from the city's other activities, modernist theory said, they could be designed by traffic engineers to carry traffic efficiently. Because suburbs and housing projects were separated from the city's other activities, they could be designed by housers to make them more livable. The city's other land uses, such as industrial areas, business parks, civic centers, and recreational areas were also supposed to be separated so each could be specially designed for its own function. The functionalists believed it was inevitable that the modern city would be built of large areas devoted to single functions and designed by experts: this was the "great scale" of modern technology.

By now, we have learned from many decades of experience that separating functions creates more problems than it solves – that it is a major cause of the problems of the contemporary American city.

Mixed Functions and Traffic

First, separating functions creates traffic congestion and parking problems.

One of the first planners to recognize this fact was Victor Gruen, who began his career by helping to invent the final element of the functionally planned city. Gruen was one of the first to build shopping in a functional superblock of own, the regional shopping center, but Gruen's work with shopping centers convinced him that single-function superblocks create massive transportation problems because they are used so unevenly during peak and slack hours.

The single function center creates traffic congestion at peak hours. For example, Gruen says that when shopping centers close for the evening, "it has been found that drivers of about 60% of all parked cars wish to leave simultaneously."[74] The investment necessary to build streets adequate to carry this much traffic would be wasted all but (about) one-half hour per day.

The single function center also uses parking wastefully because it must provide a parking lot large enough for its hours of peak use, and this parking will be underused much of the day. For example, one planner found that most of downtown Pittsburgh's parking garages operated at only 10% to 20% of capacity after 8 P.M, but there was a shortage of night-time parking in the section of Pittsburgh where the city's Symphony, Civic Light Opera, Little Theater, Carnegie Library, and other cultural facilities were located.[75] If these cultural facilities had been scattered through downtown, rather than concentrated in a separate cultural center, they would have had more convenient parking with the spaces that were already available in downtown than they had after building their own parking. They also would have avoided the traffic congestion that occurs when several performances are given on the same evening in this one cultural center.

Any large-scale single-function land use creates the same wasteful use of parking and the same congestion. An office park has parking lots that are crowded during weekdays but empty during the evening and weekends, and it has traffic congestion at the end of every week day, when most employees leave at the same time. A large park has parking lots that are packed on summer weekends but empty on weekdays during most of the year, and it has traffic congestion when everyone leaves at the end of a busy summer day.

Mixed Functions and Shopping

Second, separating functions makes it impossible for neighborhoods to support convenient and interesting shopping.

Jane Jacobs, the most influential early critic of modernist urban planning, showed that single-function planning causes what she called the "blight of dullness" for the same reason that it causes transportation problems. A neighborhood with only one "primary use" that draws people in their own right (such as housing or offices) cannot support a diversity of "secondary uses" (such as restaurants, shops, and branch libraries) that do not draw people into a neighborhood but are convenient for people already there.[76] Areas dominated by a single primary use generally have only standardized stores; for example, the typical housing-only suburb has standard supermarkets and chain restaurants on its shopping strip. By contrast, mixed-use urban neighborhoods have not only supermarkets but also small grocery stores, organic food stores, Italian bakeries, and other specialized food stores, not only McDonalds and Burger King but also ethnic and specialized restaurants. There are some people in the housing-only suburb who would shop at specialty stores if they could, but not enough to keep many of these stores in business.

In part, mixed-use urban neighborhoods support more diverse retail because they are higher density, but Jacobs showed that density alone is not enough. At the time she wrote, for example, New York's Wall-Street area had about 400,000 daily users jammed into high-rise office buildings, but it could not support interesting shops, restaurants or even a branch of the public library, because its users were virtually all office workers on the same schedule,[77] so they take advantage of these secondary uses for only a few hours each week. Thus, Wall Street's restaurants are packed beyond capacity on weekdays between noon and 2 P.M. but they are almost deserted during most of the rest of the day. Because they are so unevenly and inefficiently used, there cannot be adequate secondary uses for Wall Street's workers: only a small number of restaurants, jammed during peak hours, can support themselves on lunch-hour business alone.

Since Jacobs wrote, this principle has been widely recognized. Cities all over the country are trying to attract housing and other uses to their central business districts so that they are lively during the evenings and weekends – rather than being used Monday to Friday from nine to five and being ghost towns the rest of the time. Even the Wall Street area has added housing and become more lively than it was when Jacobs wrote.

Mixed Functions and Public Life

Third, separating functions eliminates the public life that used to give people a connection to their neighborhoods.

Jacobs argued that urban housing projects have high crime rates because they lack street life. They do not have eyes on the street, like older neighborhoods that have small stores facing the streets and apartments overlooking the streets.

In middle-class suburbs, isolation and boredom are more of a problem than crime. When you drive to a regional shopping mall, you are not likely to meet people you know, as you did in old neighborhoods where you walked to local stores. Local storekeepers had always been important public characters, who gave people a connection to their neighborhoods, but this public life has disappeared in suburbia.

During the twentieth century, America changed from a nation of towns and neighborhoods into a nation of anonymous housing tracts and shopping malls. Our cities have lost their sense of place, because they are now made up of inward-facing compounds, rather than mixed uses facing on streets. Shopping malls, office parks, and housing developments are designed as private complexes – sometimes with fences around them and security at the gate – and they turn their backs on the street.

The move from Main Street to the mall has also had a chilling effect on freedom of speech. Most of our public places are now private property, where free speech is not protected.[78] You could put up a table backing a political cause on the old neighborhood streets, but management usually will not let you put up this table in a shopping center.

Functional Planning in Suburbia

Two typical types of development in modern American suburbia provide perfect examples of the problems created by single-function planning.

In edge-city business districts in suburbia, there is traffic congestion during lunch hour that is almost as bad as the traffic congestion during commute hours, as people drive from their office parks to nearby shopping centers to run errands or to eat at a restaurant. People are likely to drive even if the shopping center is right across the street from the office park because the parking lots and arterial streets make the walk unsafe and ugly.

In residential neighborhoods in suburbia, even the people who live nearest to the shopping strip drive there instead of walking because the curving roads and cul-de-sacs make you take a long, round-about route to get to the store, even if it is nearby. Even after they get to the strip, they drive from store to store rather than parking and walking, as people do on old-fashioned Main Streets, because the shopping is set back behind parking.

As Victor Gruen said, designing an urban region as a series of single-function centers creates "enforced mobility."[79] A typical suburbanite must drive back and forth among functional centers scattered all over the landscape in order to drop the children off at school, go to the doctor, buy groceries, go to the local college for a class, and so on – driving back and forth over the same ground during the day. Consolidating all of these facilities into one "multifunctional center" would not only reduce congestion, make more efficient use of parking, and support more interesting retail; it would also eliminate the driving back and forth. The automobile trips among the single-function centers would be consolidated into a single trip to the multifunctional center, where you can walk. And the people who live in or near this urban center would rarely need to drive at all.[80]

All the early city planners believed in single-function land-use planning, but today we can see that this functional land use planning is a major cause of our transportation problems.

Comprehensive Regional Planning

When you list all the problems that have been caused by planning, as we have in this chapter, the conventional wisdom responds that they are caused by "piecemeal planning" of individual roads and individual land uses. What we need is "comprehensive regional transportation and land use planning," a single planning agency to coordinate the land uses and the transportation system of an entire region.

This was the ideal of the early regionalist planners, but the meaning of regional planning changed dramatically during the postwar period, though the catch phrase remained the same. It is useful to look at the postwar idea of regional planning, to see how much more limited it became in practice than it was in the theories of the early regionalists.

Megalopolis

Though he is almost forgotten today, Jean Gottmann was one of the most prestigious advocates of regional planning during the postwar period.[81] In his book *Megalopolis*, Gottmann described the continuous urbanized strip between Boston and Washington as the prototype of the city of the future, because the interlocking growth of these cities is caused by inevitable socio-economic forces which are operating world-wide but have progressed furthest here. Megalopolis is a result of the huge, inevitable growth of centralized administration in modern societies.[82]

Gottmann realized that Megalopolis' economic vitality also caused many difficulties, such as traffic congestion and sprawl.[83] He studied the region because "its various problems are or will be repeated, with some variance and on different scales, in most other countries,"[84] as they go through the same stage of technological development.

Gottmann believed that this region's growth caused these problems only because it occurred without any planning. For example, he said that Megalopolis' "major flows of traffic have been allowed to develop with little hindrance ... though at a cost ... of considerable money and of increasing nervous strain and physical discomfort."[85] Likewise, "The exploding suburban sprawl, the rapid changes in the distribution of population within Megalopolis, especially since 1920, are all consequences of the greater freedom of access obtained as a result of ... economic and technical achievements."[86] He did not mention how much the planners contributed to these problems.[87]

According to Gottmann, these inevitable technological developments must be molded into a workable whole through centralized planning: "Megalopolis has in the past 'muddled through' the difficulties of too much division of authority"[88] and it needs "comprehensive transportation and land-use planning." A regional planning board with authority over the entire urbanized northeastern seaboard could coordinate the development of its land uses and expansion of its transportation system. Expanding the transportation system is the key, because "'Running out of space appears to mean 'running out of easy access to desired places.' With a very good transportation system, access is not ... a matter of distance measured in miles.... "[89]

The Limits of Regional Planning

It is striking how different Gottmann's idea of regional planning is from the original ideas of Geddes, Mumford and other early regionalists.

Because they were technocrats, like Veblen, the early regionalists believed that the modern economy would inevitably be centralized and controlled by a planning board. During the 1930's, it was widely believed that that the centrally planned economy of the Soviet Union was a model for the future of all industrialized nations and that the National Resources Planning Board was the first step toward this sort of central planning authority in the United States.

In the view of early regionalists, the region's master plan involved both economic planning and city planning. The master planners would be able to reorganize production entirely, and they would understand the connections that specialist planners ignore. We have seen the regionalists believed the planners would be able to reorganize the region's economy and relocate its housing and industries to reduce cross-hauling of products, commuting, and other unnecessary transportation.

This sort of command-and-control planning seemed plausible when the earliest planners wrote, because the economy was relatively simple then. For example, Edward Bellamy said that managing his socialist society would be "so simple and depending on principles so obvious and easily applied, that the functionaries at Washington to whom it is trusted require to be nothing more than men of fair ability."[90] Lenin still believed in this nineteenth century ideal, and he said that the administration of a socialist society would become so simple that even a shoemaker could run the economy.[91]

Today, everyone knows that this sort of command-and-control economic planning does not work. The Soviet Union and the other command-and-control economies of eastern Europe collapsed because they were economically inefficient and backward. The world has changed since Lincoln Steffans looked at Lenin's planned economy in Russia and said "I have seen the future, and it works."[92]

Command-and-control planning does not work because today's technology is so complex that decisions have to be made by people who have the relevant expertise – people within the industry itself. No master planning board could possibly deal with all of the information and understand all of the branches of knowledge needed to plan the industrial, agricultural, energy, transportation, and urban development of an entire economy.

Instead of centralized planning, what are we need are ways of breaking up the questions planners deal with into pieces of manageable size. As the Nobel Prize-winning economist Herbert Simon said: "the mere existence of a mass of data is not a sufficient reason for collecting it into a single, comprehensive information system. Indeed, the problem is quite the opposite: of finding a way of factoring decision problems in order to relate the several components to their respective relevant data sources.[93]

Today, the goal is not to combine all decision making under a single master-planning board but to unhook each decision from the others so that the body of information that a given team of specialized planners must deal with remains manageable. The old idea of command-and-control planning, with a single planning board managing the entire economy, has been replaced by the idea that each set of planners must be autonomous, because it must make decisions in terms of its own expertise, and that each set of planners must fit itself into the larger picture by projecting and accommodating future trends of the economy as a whole.

This is how city planning actually developed in postwar America. As we have seen, the Chicago school were the first to develop a methodology that the planners could use to project economic and demographic trends, so they could provide the housing, the retail space, or the transportation that future growth would require. Now that centrally planned economies have collapsed, it should be clear that the old idea of command-and-control planning must be replaced with this newer type of project-and-accommodate planning.

What is a Region?

Because the nature of planning changed, the concept of a planning region also changed.

The early regionalists thought of the region as an economically diverse, well balanced and relatively self-sufficient area. The Tennessee Valley Authority, developing an entire watershed as a single unit, was their prime example of how a natural region could be developed to bring multiple local economic benefits, as its dams provided flood control, water, electricity, and recreation. The early regionalists believed a central planning board would control the entire economy of each self-sufficient region to provide local economic benefits.

But the early regionalists never developed any method for determining the boundaries of a region. They said that planners would design the regions to minimize transportation of raw materials and finished goods, but in reality, you would have to draw very different regional boundaries to minimize the transportation used to produce and distribute milk, textiles, energy, and steel. Sometimes they identified the region with some obvious natural feature, such as the Tennessee River valley, but the boundaries of natural features can be very different from the boundaries needed to create self-sufficient economic regions.

Benton MacKaye, an early regionalist who was a practical planner, defined a region as, "a rounded unit of development" that "corresponds with some natural scheme of flowage – of water, commodity or population."[94] During the postwar period, regional planning agencies were established to deal with many different types of "flowage" that cut across political jurisdictions, and these regions' boundaries were all different. Regional water development agencies administer watersheds. Regional air quality agencies administer air basins. Regional transportation agencies administer metropolitan areas that need unified transportation planning. In each case, the region is defined to correspond to the particular form of "flowage" that one set of planners is interested in – of water, air pollutants, or traffic. The sort of integrated regions that the early planners expected never appeared; instead, there is a patchwork of overlapping, single-function regions.[95]

In the real world, "comprehensive regional land-use and transportation planning" clearly cannot control the entire economy, as the early regionalists had hoped. It must be coordinated with the rest of the economy in the same way that any other specialized planning is: the regional planning agency must project the future population and economic growth of the region and then design the regional zoning map and transportation system needed to accommodate this growth. Project-and-accommodate planning has replaced the top-down command-and-control planning that the early regionalists believed in.

Gottmann took this narrow view of comprehensive regional land-use and transportation planning. He used the old technocratic rhetoric when he called for totally centralized planning, but he busily projected the economic trends that the planners must accommodate. He called these trends inevitable, because they are outside of the city planners' control.

Gottmann obviously did not have the radical edge of the early regionalists. They wanted to reduce the need for transportation by simplifying the economy and promoting local production, and they were also suspicious of consumerism and economic growth.[96] By contrast, Gottmann wanted to provide more transportation to accommodate economic growth, and he believed consumerism was a good thing even if it was wasteful: "A certain kind of planned waste is healthful for an economy of abundance in an industrialized society ... as long as it follows and supports the general tide of growth and progress."[97]

The early regionalists wanted to change the modern economy. Gottman and other postwar regionalists wanted to accommodate the modern economy.

Chapter 4
New Traditional Urbanism

A political movement against modernist planning began during the 1960s, but this movement remained purely negative for decades. It was a movement against freeways, against urban sprawl, and against redevelopment projects.

During the last couple of decades, critics of modernism have begun working positively to rebuild our cities. The New Urbanists and the smart growth movement are building new neighborhoods and rebuilding entire regions in a neo-traditional style. But as practicing planners, they work with the tools that are available – and that means that they use top-down planning.

They have not looked at the relation between planning and politics in broader theoretical terms. Today's planners and environmentalists recognize that the worst problems of American cities are caused by the suburban sprawl, the freeways, the shopping malls and the office parks produced by modernist planning – but they still believe we need more planning to solve these problems.

Resistance Against Modernism

The earliest and best book criticizing modernist planning was Jane Jacobs *The Death and Life of Great American Cities*, published in 1961 and filled with ideas that are still fresh. Jacobs was the one who showed that the modernist emperor had no clothes: everyone knew that the freeways, the centers for the performing arts, and the housing projects made our cities uglier and less livable, and Jacobs explained why. She changed everyone's thinking about planning by saying that the modernist planners' ideal – what she called "The Radiant Garden City" – was the source of many of the problems of modern American cities.

Instead of the "great scale" of modernist planning, she valued traditional city design – with small blocks, with fine-grained diversity of uses, and with housing and business oriented toward the street – because it made cities safer, more convenient, and more neighborly.

Jacobs lived in Greenwich Village when citizens were battling Robert Moses' plans to replace the West Village with a housing project, to build a road through Washington Square Park, and to build a Cross-Manhattan Expressway just to the south of the Village. She knew the public characters who held the neighborhood together and helped it fight these plans effectively. Much of her book is based on her observations of her neighborhood and of other neighborhoods like it.

Beginning in the 1960s, there was a political reaction against modernist planning. There was a movement to stop urban freeways and urban renewal in order to save existing urban neighborhoods, which Jane Jacobs was part of, and there was a parallel movement to stop shopping malls and suburban sprawl in order to save existing small towns, which was most successful in Vermont.

It was not until the 1990s that the movement against modernist planning began to emphasize positive proposals. In addition to working against modernist projects that threaten traditional neighborhoods, it began working for projects that would build neighborhoods and entire regions in a neo-traditional mold.

On the micro scale, the New Urbanists began building new neighborhoods and rebuilding existing neighborhoods using traditional neighborhood design as their model. They became influential after the Congress for the New Urbanism was founded in 1993.

On the macro scale, the smart growth movement began to rebuild entire regions by using the traditional pattern of transit oriented development as their model. Parris Glendenning popularized the phrase "smart growth" after being elected governor of Maryland in 1994, and Portland, Oregon, became the nation's prime example of smart growth.

These two movements reinforced each other. The New Urbanists support smart growth, though as practicing developers they often have to build where there is no transit. The smart growth movement uses New Urbanist principles to design transit-oriented developments that encourage people to walk to local services and to the transit stations, as people did in the old railroad and streetcar suburbs built 100 years ago.

These two movements both use top-down planning to build old-fashioned neighborhoods. The most famous New Urbanist neighborhoods were designed by planners who wrote urban and architectural codes that controlled their development very tightly. The smart growth movement calls for comprehensive regional land-use and transportation planning, to build transit systems and to require developers to concentrate development near transit nodes. Though they grew out of the movement to stop modernist planning and preserve old neighborhoods and towns, they take it for granted that they themselves must use planning.

The New Urbanism

The New Urbanism, the most important movement in urban design today, has revived traditional neighborhood design. It rejects the modernist idea that cities should be made up of inward-facing superblocks, which have interior streets designed for local access and are surrounded by arterial streets for through traffic. Instead, it calls for a street system with small blocks, for development that is oriented toward the street rather than facing away from it, and for a variety of different land uses within walking distance of each other. This sort of design works for both pedestrians and automobiles, while modernist design does not work for pedestrians.

Principles of New Urbanism

The most famous New Urbanist developments are suburbs that are designed like the American towns or suburbs of a century ago, such as Andres Duany's Seaside and Kentlands. Because these are entire neighborhoods built from the ground up, they are striking illustrations of New Urbanist principles.

These New Urbanist suburbs have a continuous street system, similar to the street grid of older cities and towns. To avoid the monotony of the grid, streets can be curved slightly and can terminate in T-intersections, but they must be designed to allow people to walk. By contrast with conventional suburbs, which have streets that are cul-de-sacs or have extreme curves, the streets in New Urbanist towns are direct enough that it is possible either to drive or to walk to nearby shopping.

To promote walking and to conserve land, New Urbanist suburbs are built at higher density than conventional suburbs – 8 or 10 units per acre instead of the 4 units per acre typical of suburbia, a density that is high enough to support some shopping within walking distance of most homes.

In addition, New Urbanist suburbs have narrow streets, in order to save land and to slow traffic. Conventional suburban streets have 12 foot traffic lanes and 10 foot parking lanes. New Urbanist suburbs have a maximum of 10 foot traffic lanes and 8 foot parking lanes – which was conventional street design during the early twentieth century – and often they have much narrower streets. Andres Duany has designed some streets as narrow as 19 feet wide, with two way traffic and on-street parking on one side: he calls these "yield streets," because when two cars meet that are going in opposite directions, there is not enough room for both of them, and one must yield the right of way to the other by pulling into the parking lane. Needless to say, these 19-foot-wide streets slow traffic considerably. Conventional suburban streets also have wide turning radiuses at intersections, which allows traffic to make turns at high speeds, while New Urbanist suburbs have tight turning radiuses at intersections, which force drivers to slow down when they turn and which also give pedestrians a shorter distance to cross.

New Urbanist suburbs have a variety of land uses within walking distance of each other. Some streets have only housing, but there are also shopping streets within walking distance of those homes. Ideally, there should be transit stops within walking distance of homes and businesses.

In addition to their continuous street grids, higher densities, and mixture of uses, New Urbanist neighborhoods have development that is oriented toward the sidewalk to make it more pleasant for people to walk.

Their shopping streets are designed like traditional Main Streets, with stores facing the sidewalk and housing or offices above. Off-street parking is behind the stores, so it does not interrupt the continuous store frontages that pedestrians walk by. These streets also have on-street parking, which makes it more pleasant for people to walk by acting as a buffer between the sidewalk and the traffic, and which also slows traffic on the main street when cars stop to park. On this sort of street, the stores help bring business to each other: after shopping in one store, people often walk up and down the street just to look at the other people and at the store windows. Of course, this design is just the opposite of the suburban strip mall – where the stores are set back from the sidewalk, where parking is in front of the stores, and where no on-street parking is allowed in order to speed up traffic on the arterial street – which is very unpleasant for pedestrians.

Residential streets are also oriented toward the sidewalk. Homes have small setbacks and front yards, and they have front porches and entrances facing the sidewalk to make them more welcoming to pedestrians. Garages are in the back, with access through a driveway next to the house or through a rear alley. In some cases, there are second units above the garages, to increase density further and to provide a variety of different types of housing for a diverse population: the small rental units are appropriate for elderly people, for example, while the houses are appropriate for families. New Urbanists use the name "snout houses" to describe conventional suburban houses, which have huge garage doors facing the street while the main door for people is inconspicuous; these houses are welcoming to cars but not to pedestrians.

This sort of street design certainly works better for pedestrians than conventional suburban design. The shopping streets become a center of the community, as they were in traditional neighborhoods. People get to know their neighbors because they see them walking through the neighborhood to go shopping and they see them at the local shopping street.

Walter Kulash, a New Urbanist traffic engineer, argues that this sort of street design also works better for automobiles than conventional suburban design. Because conventional suburbs put all the cars on a few large arterial streets, they need traffic signals with left-turn phases, which make drivers wait at intersections; there is almost never a gap in all of the three or four lanes of traffic going in the opposite direction that would allow a left turn. By contrast, Kulash says, when you disperse cars on a grid of many small streets, there are often gaps in the one lane of traffic going in the opposite direction that allow left turns, so there is no need for left-turn signals.[98] There is some truth to what Kulash says, but it is also true that New Urbanist street design makes people drive more slowly than conventional suburban street design, so it makes it less convenient to drive long distances to regional malls or big-box centers. Yet New Urbanist street design undoubtedly does make it easier to drive to local shopping – which is nerve wracking in conventional suburbs, where you cannot get to the local store without driving on a six or eight-lane road where traffic travels at 40 or 50 miles per hour.

Because its best known projects are suburbs, with the sort of design that we just described, there is a popular misconception that New Urbanism is just a method of designing suburbs differently. Actually, it is a traditional approach to the design of urban neighborhoods and small towns as well as suburbs.

Many urban projects have been proposed by New Urbanist designers. One of the earliest New Urbanist projects was Peter Calthorpe's proposal for development in Brooklyn in the form of a traditional neighborhood, with streets of traditional urban row houses and higher density commercial streets, but this project was stopped by neighborhood opposition.[99] Another New Urbanist development with an urban feel is Liberty Harbor in Jersey City. The HOPE VI designs to rebuild urban housing projects were also strongly influenced by New Urbanism. In fact, the Charter of the New Urbanism says as its first goal, "We stand for the restoration of existing urban centers and towns...."[100]

The New Urbanists use the same principles of traditional urban design in urban neighborhoods that they use in suburbs. They reject the modernists' idea that we should build inward-facing single-use superblocks surrounded by arterial streets. Instead, they build an old-fashioned continuous street grid with small blocks. They orient development to the sidewalk, to encourage people to walk among different uses. They do not let parking lots disrupt the pedestrian feel of the street; instead, they hide parking behind buildings or they structure parking into buildings, to create pedestrian-friendly facades facing the sidewalk.

Planned New Urbanism

When Andres Duany designed Seaside, Florida, some realtors said no one would buy there: why would anyone want a house with a such a small lot when they could buy one with a much larger lot in a conventional suburb for the same price? But in fact, Seaside was tremendously successful, because people liked the feeling of community they had in a town where they could walk.

New Urbanism soon became so successful that *Emerging Trends in Real Estate*, the country's most respected real estate forecast, said that the two most important trends in real estate investment are twenty-four-hour downtowns and New Urbanist neighborhoods:

> "the age-old concept of living in a town setting … suddenly has renewed attraction for an increasing number of American suburb dwellers – people who find themselves dependent on a car to go anywhere or do anything. Sample the attitudes of suburbanites today and you'll find a growing number who think their lifestyle is becoming more difficult and less appealing.[101]

Many cities and towns have adopted New Urbanist zoning laws, which take two forms. Some are like conventional zoning ordinances, except that they allow smaller lot sizes and have smaller setback requirements. Others are like the urban codes first developed by Andres Duany, which are sometimes called form-based codes. Miami recently became the first large city to adopt a form-based code.

New Urbanists prefer these form-based codes to conventional zoning. Zoning laws are typically proscriptive, telling developers what they cannot do, while form-based codes are more prescriptive, telling developers what they should do. For example, conventional zoning ordinances have a minimum setback requirement; developers cannot build beyond this setback line, but they can set back buildings further than the line. By contrast, form-based codes have a build-to line;

development must be built at this distance from the sidewalk. Likewise, conventional zoning ordinances have a maximum height, but if the maximum height on Main Street is five stories, a developer could still build a one-story drive-in there. Form-based codes have both a maximum and a minimum height; Main Street might have a minimum height of three stories and a maximum height of five stories, so new buildings must fit in with its scale. The code would have different sets of guidelines to define the building types allowed on shopping streets, streets of single-family houses, streets of row houses, and so on.

In addition to these form-based urban codes, which control the massing and location of buildings, many New Urbanist developments also have architectural codes, which specify materials that may be used, the roof overhangs that are required, and other design elements that give the entire development a consistent architectural style.[102]

Piecemeal New Urbanism

The best known New Urbanist developments are projects whose design is controlled by a single planning firm. The planners might design the entire project, or they might lay out the street system and create the urban and architectural codes that determine how the entire project will look. Many people identify New Urbanism with this sort of top-down, controlled design.

However, the basic principles of New Urbanism have also influenced many small piecemeal developments. A few decades ago, small developments typically emulated the "project" style even if they were on traditional street grids: they were set back behind parking lots or plazas, and they turned their backs to the street; but today, it has become common for small developments to be oriented to the street. A few decades ago, cities were busy removing parking and making streets one-way to speed up traffic; but today, it has become common for cities to try to slow down traffic to make streets more pleasant for pedestrians.

These piecemeal developments tend to be overlooked, because they are not as striking visually as entire developments in a consistent style, but they should also be considered an important part of New Urbanism

Many downtowns are being revived using traditional design. The best known is Fort Worth, Texas, where the revival has been spurred by the Bass family, one of the nation's richest families. The Bass's earliest projects were modernist designs, including two 38-story office buildings clad in reflective glass, and they were planning to build a modernist performing arts complex, nicknamed Lincoln Center Southwest, until that project was stopped by the collapse of the state's oil and real estate values in the 1980s. However, they were also renovating the area's old brick buildings, and soon they changed their plans: instead of developing modernist office towers, they began developing new buildings in the same style as downtown's traditional buildings, with a mix of housing, shopping and entertainment as well as offices. This redevelopment culminated in 1998 with the opening of Bass Hall, the first American concert hall to be oriented toward the street, rather than isolated in a center for the performing arts, since Severence Hall was built in Cleveland more than 65 years earlier. Instead of Lincoln Center, the model was Carnegie Hall; on opening day, Edward Bass told a reporter that Bass Hall "is designed to fit into the urban fabric as much as Carnegie."[103]

Though Fort Worth is the most famous example, old downtowns are being revived in much the same way all over the country. For example, Berkeley, California, had no privately developed housing built in its downtown for over sixty years – from the beginning of the depression until the 1990s. During that time, a few faceless modernist office buildings were built in downtown, and one apartment building of public housing for the elderly was built a block from downtown, with a blank wall behind landscaping facing the main street. But since 1990, over a dozen mixed use buildings have been built or are scheduled to be built in downtown Berkeley or within a block of it, and they all have ground floor shopping that faces directly on the sidewalk with several floors of housing above – the same design that was common when downtown was first being developed, a century earlier.

The move back to downtown is a national trend. A study by the Brookings Institution and the Fannie Mae Foundation found that all of the twenty-four cities studied forecast growth of population in downtown, a reversal of the trend that started after World War II. For example, the number of people living downtown is expected to quadruple in Houston, to more than triple in Cleveland, to almost triple in Denver, and to increase by one-third in Chicago.[104]

Many cities are also building traditional urban shopping streets instead of the auto-oriented strip malls of a few decades ago. In cities all over the United States, major streets in neighborhoods built during the first half of the nineteenth century were never developed fully. During their early years, they were developed with a few traditional urban buildings, with housing above shopping, but during the twentieth century, they were filled in with strip-mall style development. Now some of these underused sites are being redeveloped, and the gas stations, parking lots, and fast-food stands are being replaced with housing above shopping that faces the sidewalk. If the trend continues for a few more decades, these streets will end up looking like people expected they would when their earliest buildings were built, a century ago.

The new baseball fields that fit into the existing street system are also excellent examples of piecemeal New Urbanism. Until recently, new baseball fields were invariably built in project style, surrounded by arterial streets and by a sea of parking. Oriole Park at Camden Yards in Baltimore, which opened in 1992, started a national trend of building old-fashioned baseball parks that are integrated into their cities' street systems. Since then, baseball fields in this style have been built in Cleveland, Denver, San Francisco, Toledo, Oklahoma City, Akron Ohio, Troy New York, Casper Wyoming, and other cities.

San Francisco's AT&T Park is pure New Urbanist design, though it was done without top-down control by New Urbanist planners. There was no urban code that forced them to build facing the sidewalk, and no architectural code that forced them to build a traditional brick building. There was no comprehensive regional land-use and transportation planning, but they did find a vacant site that is near downtown and well served by public transit. The field is unique because it had to fit into this odd site: it has a short right-field fence, and people in small boats wait in the bay during games to get baseballs that are hit over this fence – a real addition to the character of San Francisco.

AT&T Park is also very successful in terms of transportation because it had to fit into this odd site, where there was no room for parking. It is near downtown San Francisco and public transportation. It is right on the street, so people walk to it, and it has helped revive the entire area around it. It makes use of nearby parking lots, but it has little enough parking that only about 50% of the people who attend games come by car.

It is not likely that comprehensive planning would have produced a field with as much character and as much use of clean transportation as AT&T Park; the planners would have set aside enough land area to allow a standard size right field, and they could not have gotten away with providing so little parking.

New Urbanist towns designed by one planning firm in a consistent architectural style are better known, but piecemeal New Urbanism is esthetically superior in some ways. The projects designed by one planning firm are important theoretically because they have established the basic principles of New Urbanism, and they are more striking esthetically because all their buildings are consistent architecturally. But maybe this striking consistency is actually an esthetic weakness: modernists criticize New Urbanism by saying it looks unreal, like a stage set or a theme-park. These controlled developments do not have as much variety as you find in real traditional neighborhoods – including the occasional inconsistencies and bad architecture.

This esthetic problem should become clear as New Urbanism becomes even more popular. For example, one developer of a suburb in Arizona might decide that he likes beach towns in Florida and use an urban code and architectural code to imitate one. And the developer of the suburb at the next off ramp, who likes neo-classical neighborhoods, might imitate a Georgian-style suburb of Washington, DC. And the developer of the suburb at the next off-ramp might imitate a Victorian village in the style of nineteenth-century San Francisco. Esthetic clashes like these are bound to occur when architectural styles are imposed on entire developments – and they will draw everyone's attention to the clash between the ideal of small-scale, small-town development and the reality of large-scale suburban development, where one planner controls the design of every building in a subdivision.

At some time in the future, after we have rebuilt the old downtowns and old shopping streets, which were blighted with parking lots and drive-ins that developers are now filling in with traditional buildings, we may decide that these piecemeal developments are the best examples of New Urbanism.

At any rate, the most common criticisms of the New Urbanism would be deflected if we made it clear that this sort of piecemeal redevelopment is one part New Urbanism. No one would be able to say that New Urbanist design looks like a stage set. And no one would be able to say that New Urbanists just care about the suburbs, because these small-scale New Urbanist developments are generally in older downtowns or in the shopping streets of old neighborhoods. Most critics of New Urbanism do not realize that it is an approach to urban design – with a continuous street system, buildings oriented to the street, and mixed uses in proximity to each other – that has become popular in small-scale developments as well as in the better known large-scale developments.

Because New Urbanists want to create developments that look like traditional towns, they should celebrate the developments that are being in built in a piecemeal way, as traditional towns were, rather than focusing on developments built as unified projects.

Smart Growth

The conventional wisdom says that we need comprehensive land-use and transportation planning at the regional scale, in addition to New Urbanist planning on the neighborhood scale. There should be a single agency that plans the region's transportation system and land uses, so it can lay out public transit lines and cluster new development in walkable neighborhoods located near transit stops.

There have been a number of attempts at regional land use and transportation planning in the United States, which range from relatively democratic processes based on public envisioning in Seattle to top-down processes dictated by the state in Florida.[105] To see the range of possibilities, we will look at the most and the least democratic examples of regional planning, Portland, Oregon, and Atlanta, Georgia.

The Portland Region

Though Portland is the most democratic regional planning we have had in the United States, even in this best case, there are limits on how much control the public can have over the planners.

In 1973, Oregon passed a law requiring all of its cities and towns to create Urban Growth Boundary (UGB) lines: cities had to project how much land would be needed for future development, draw a line that could contain all that development, and forbid new development beyond the line. In 1979, the Portland metropolitan area adopted a final UGB and also established a regional governing body named Metro.

The UGB was meant to protect open space, and the state law said nothing about how cities should be designed within the urban growth boundary. The Portland region addressed this issue itself after the Oregon Department of Transportation (ODOT) proposed a freeway named the Western Bypass in Washington county, where the region's most rapidly growing suburbs were located. This freeway would have just made sprawl and automobile dependency worse, but Metro accepted ODOT's proposal and included this highway in its Regional Transportation Plan.

Beginning in 1991, an environmental group named 1000 Friends of Oregon opposed this freeway by developing an alternative plan, which it called Making the Land Use, Transportation, Air Quality Connection – or LUTRAQ for short. This plan proposed new light-rail and bus service, with Transit Oriented Development (TOD) clustered around the transit stations. To establish TOD as a feasible alternative, 1000 Friends did demographic and market research to show that Washington County was not providing enough multifamily housing to meet market demand. It also developed a computer model to measure how many trips could be shifted from automobiles to alternative modes by TOD. This model was called the Pedestrian Environment Factor (PEF), but it was later replaced by a model developed by Metro, named the Urban Index, which was based on the density of jobs and density of street intersections, which was found to be simpler and more accurate than the PEF.

During the environmental review process, 1000 Friends got the LUTRAC plan included as one of the alternatives considered in the

Environmental Impact Statement for the freeway. The EIS found that, compared with the freeway, LUTRAC resulted in 18% less highway congestion and 6% to 8.7% less air pollution. After studying the bypass and four other alternatives, the analysis found that the LUTRAC alternative was the only alternative apart from the no-build alternative that complied with the federal Clean Air Act. As a result of this environmental study, Metro killed the bypass and adopted the LUTRAC alternative in 1996.

At the same time that the battle over the Western Bypass was being fought, Metro was also reviewing the UGB and developing the Region 2040 Plan to accommodate projected growth during the coming decades. After projecting job and population growth, polling the public to see what it wanted, creating visualizations of three alternative scenarios for the region, and getting feedback from the public about this visualization, Metro ultimately adopted a plan for the entire region that was similar to the LUTRAC alternative. The 2040 Functional Plan adopted in 1996 added new light-rail, high-capacity bus lines, and feeder bus lines, and it concentrated new development around transit stops.[106] The plan also required at least eight street intersections per mile in new and redeveloping areas, in order to create street systems with the small blocks that make neighborhoods walkable.

The planners found that, compared with a base case that simply continued past development patterns, this alternative reduced Vehicle Miles Traveled per capita by 20% and improved air quality.[107] Because of these policies, transit use was projected to increase from 8% to 13% of commute trips by 2040, and automobile use was projected to decline by almost 11%, as new pedestrian and transit-oriented neighborhoods are built.

This planning has made Portland a national model. Even the *Wall Street Journal*, which is not usually known for its environmentalism, has called Portland an "Urban Mecca," which has become so livable that it draws planners from all over the country to study it. Portland's downtown businesses have thrived, though no new parking has been added in downtown; some of the new customers come by transit – two downtown streets have been closed to cars and converted to transit malls – and some live in the new housing that has been built downtown. Portland also has some of the liveliest local shopping streets on the west coast; refugees from Los Angeles are sometimes shocked to find that their neighborhood streets are so interesting that they actually feel like going out in the evening just to take a walk.[108]

Of all the metropolitan areas that have begun to use regional planning, Portland has been the most democratic by far. An activist group challenged the regional planning agency when it approved a freeway, and ultimately changed the regional plan. The new regional plan was developed using an envisioning process that gave people a chance to think about alternatives visually, so they could decide which alternative was the way they wanted to live.

But even in Portland, the democratic decision about how people want to live is trumped by technical decisions that the planners must make. To challenge the Western Bypass, the activist group had to hire planners who developed an alternative and did complex technical studies about its impacts. As we have seen, the LUTRAC plan was chosen over the freeway because it was found to produce 18% less highway congestion and 6 to 8.7% less air pollution, and because it was the only build alternative that complied with the federal Clean Air Act – and these are all technical questions that planners must answer, not political questions about how people want to live.

Despite extensive public input, the 2040 Plan was ultimately based on similar technical considerations. Citizens influenced the overall direction of the plan, but the planners had the final say.

The Atlanta Region

By contrast with Portland's relatively democratic approach, Atlanta, Georgia, is an example of a completely top-down and technocratic approach to regional planning.

Its plan was developed by the state in response to a federal mandate. By law, metropolitan regions can lose their federal transportation funding if they do not spend it in a way that conforms with the regional air quality plan prepared under the federal Clean Air Act. Atlanta was one of the nation's most serious air quality nonattainment areas, and when the clean-air deadline approached in the late 1990s, Atlanta was faced with the possibility of losing more than $1 billion in federal transportation funding by 2005.

As a result, the Georgia legislature passed a law in 1998 setting up the Georgia Regional Transportation Authority (GRTA) with almost total control over transportation and land-use decisions in the 13-county Atlanta metropolitan area. GRTA can tell the state transportation authority not to build a highway; it can tell a county not to allow a new shopping center; it can build public transportation in any of the counties under its jurisdiction and force the county to pay for it by threatening to take away its state financing. This regional planning agency is a 15-member board headed by the governor, who can appoint and dismiss all the other members at will. Roy Barnes was governor when the law was passed, and at the time, some people joked that GRTA stood for "Give Roy Total Authority."[109]

This approach to regionalism is completely technocratic. Regional planning began because federal air quality planners required Atlanta to reduce air pollution. Planning was not based on any political discussion of how people want to live, as it is in Portland and other regions that have used envisioning processes. Yet air pollution is a technical problem and is subject to technological fixes: in a few decades, we will all have hybrid cars, which produce 80% less urban air pollution than today's cars. At that point, a region like Atlanta – where there has been top-down regional planning with no political discussion about what type of city people want to live in – will go right back to auto dependency and sprawl.

What's Wrong with Regional Planning

Portland is undeniably a model showing that we can make American cities more livable by building transit rather than freeways, and by designing pedestrian-oriented neighborhoods around the transit stops. The question is whether the best way to move in this direction is by using regional planning.

Top-down regional planning has many problems because it deals with complex technical issues that must ultimately be decided by the planners.

First, top-down regional planning tends to be undemocratic. Even in Portland, where a citizen's group challenged the regional planners, they were able to succeed only by hiring their own set of planners and showing that their plan was better on technical grounds. In reality, their plan appealed to people because it was a vision of a better way to live, but the final decision about which plan to adopt was not based on people's ideas about how they wanted to live; it was based on the planners' calculations of projected air quality and traffic congestion. Citizens were able to have an effect because Portland was a relatively small city, with about 1,400,000 people in the entire metropolitan area. Citizens would have much less power if there were centralized planning for the entire Los Angeles-Long Beach region, or the entire New York-Newark region.

Second, top-down regional planning gives people less individual choice about how they want to live. The type of housing that is produced depends on the technical requirements of the plan: the planners must decide what mix of freestanding houses, row houses, and apartments is needed to reduce air pollution and traffic congestion to manageable levels, not what mix of housing people want to live in. Today, after many decades of government policy favoring single-family houses, we undoubtedly are giving people more choice by building apartment houses and row houses. But if the top-down planning of the past skewed housing supply toward single-family houses, should we replace it with more top-down planning that could ultimately skew the supply in the opposite direction?

Third, top-down regional planning is not effective enough. Even in Portland, where a strong environmentalist movement has given the region the political will to stop the Western Bypass freeway, to create transit malls downtown, and to tear down the Harbor Drive freeway, per capita automobile use was projected to decrease by less than 11% in the 50 years between 1990 and 2040. Though this reduction in driving is a significant accomplishment, the change is very slow compared with past growth of automobile use – the average American drives about four times as much now as in 1950 – and we will need faster change than this to deal with energy shortages and global warming during the coming decades.

(The changes in Atlanta are much slower than in Portland, of course, because they want to reduce automobile use just enough to meet government air quality standards. In fact, their main motive for regional planning is to keep getting federal funding for more freeways.)

Regionally planned transit-oriented development reduces automobile use slowly because most people still drive to distant shopping centers and jobs. As long as they can get right on the freeway and drive to a regional shopping mall, many people ignore the pedestrian-oriented shopping in their own neighborhoods and go to big-box discount stores; the local hardware store cannot compete with prices at the Home Depot. It should be clear that transit-oriented development, though necessary, is not sufficient to cure automobile dependency: most American neighborhoods in 1945 were pedestrian and transit-oriented and filled with local shopping, but within a few decades, many of the local stores were driven out of business by competition from new shopping centers surrounded by parking lots.

Finally, top-down regional planning is a confused mixture of command-and-control planning with project-and-accommodate planning. The command-and-control planning extends only to land use and transportation issues, while the planners must project and accommodate the region's economic growth, population growth and so on.

Today's advocates of regional planning do not have a consistent theoretical approach. During the 1930s, the regionalists had a consistent view of economic and urban planning: they believed that urban planning was one element of comprehensive economic planning, and they believed that the shift from a market economy to a planned economy would solve the problems caused by growth. By contrast, today's regional planning is a narrow approach to dealing with symptoms of urban growth, and it does not have any vision of larger changes needed in the economy. It wants a bit of command-and-control planning over physical development, but no one believes any longer that there should be a larger shift from a market economy to a command-and-control planned economy.

In Portland, the political movement against the Western Bypass had a vision of a different way to live – a vision of pedestrian oriented neighborhoods that not only do less damage to the environment but are also more interesting and more attractive places than conventional suburban sprawl development. But this political movement could go only so far because it was working within the EIS process and the regional planning process – and, even more important, it could go only so far because it limited urban growth using the old, unwieldy method of command-and-control planning. This movement was successful because the region has had the political will to tear down Harbor Drive freeway, to make two downtown streets into transit malls, and to stop the Western Bypass. It could be much more successful if it focused less on planning and more on direct political limits on urban growth.

Chapter 5
Political Limits on Urban Growth

Why do we need all this planning to build cities that look like cities did a century ago, before there were any urban planners?

Simply doing away with planning will not let us build traditional neighborhoods, because technology has changed since the old neighborhoods that we admire were built. If we eliminated planning, developers would still build office parks, shopping malls, and suburban tract housing, even if the zoning laws did not force them to. That is why the conventional wisdom says that more planning is inevitable to deal with new problems of modern cities.

But we can reduce the need for planning by putting political limits on urban growth. We can directly limit effects of modernization that make planning seem necessary and inevitable.

First, we can limit the scale of development. We can limit the maximum land area that a development can cover, as we now limit height and ground coverage. The planners will still have to create a street system with small blocks, but these blocks can be filled in with individual small-scale developments.

Second, we can limit use of the automobile. One very effective way to do this is to reduce the speed limit for automobiles, which would shift longer trips to public transportation, would stop sprawl, and would shorten the average trip length.

This chapter will look at different ways that cities would be built if we had different political limits on scale and on speed, with these limits in effect during the entire time that the cities are being developed. These are not proposals for changing our existing cities.

They are models used in a thought experiment, to show that political limits on growth could let people choose what sort of city they live in, and to show that political limits on growth are essential to creating livable cities.

Today's New Urbanists and regionalists are practical planners, so their most striking accomplishments have been based on the biggest opportunities for practical planning: entire suburban developments and comprehensive regional plans. By contrast, this chapter asks a theoretical question: if we are building a region from scratch, what is the best way to create a traditional urban pattern – best politically, esthetically, and environmentally?

Limiting Scale

With conventional zoning, cities, suburbs and towns try to control their character by controlling which land uses are allowed. Instead, this section suggests that they can control their character by using the appropriate scale when they lay out their street systems and by limiting the scale of development.

To create the proper scale, cities should begin by laying out a street system with small blocks. Cities should follow Portland's rule of at least eight street connections per mile; research in Portland found that small blocks are a key variable in determining how pedestrian and transit-friendly neighborhoods are.[110] In addition, streets should be relatively narrow, with a 10-foot-wide traffic lanes and 8-foot-wide parking lanes at the most, to slow traffic and save land. They should also have adequate sidewalks, at least 10 feet wide. Other features of street design might depend on climate: for example, in a cold and windy location, the street grid should be oriented diagonally to the prevailing winds, so rows of buildings shelter streets from the wind.

Cities should require new developments to fit into these traditional urban blocks, rather than being built in oversized superblocks like suburban shopping centers, office parks and housing tracts. Developments may be larger than one block, but they should be designed around the street grid and should retain all the streets.

New York's Rockefeller Center is an example where this was done very well: it is a large complex that not only fits into the existing street grid but also adds a new internal street. (When large developments are built, the city might specify the locations of the streets but leave it to developers to build the sidewalks and streets within their developments.)

When it lays out the street system, the city must also decide on the location of transit lines. Some streets will have to be wide enough to have room for exclusive bus or light-rail lanes, and some streets may have to be laid out around commuter rail lines.

In addition to laying out a street system on the appropriate scale, the city can control the character of development by setting a maximum height and maximum land area for new development.

Conventional zoning laws already limit building height. It is best to set height limits as a number of stories, as traditional cities did, rather than as a number of feet, as most modern zoning laws do, to make the streetscape more interesting by creating minor variations in buildings' height.

Conventional zoning laws also limit how much of the site can be developed, and we need some maximum on ground coverage to prevent developers from building on 100% of the property, overshadowing the neighboring lots, and creating neighborhoods without light or air, like nineteenth-century tenements. A rough limit would probably be enough for most locations. A city can vary the character of different neighborhoods with different limits on height and ground coverage.

Most suburban zoning laws go much too far in limiting height and ground coverage, because they are trying to keep densities down to levels needed to accommodate automobile dependency. However, it is also possible to limit height and ground coverage just enough to promote the traditional densities of walkable neighborhoods.

Though conventional zoning laws just limit height and ground coverage, experience should make it clear that we also need to limit the total land area that a single builder can develop. Suburban shopping centers, office parks, and housing developments usually have very low height limits and ground coverages, but they are oppressively monotonous – with acres of one-story buildings in a sea of parking.

We can eliminate this sort of large-scale single-use development by limiting the land area that a single builder can develop; lots larger than this area would have to be subdivided and developed independently by multiple builders, each developer building around the street system that the city has laid out.

Controlling a City's Character

By looking at a few examples, we can see how a city can control its character by limiting the maximum height and land area of development – but we must bear in mind that these limits are meant to be used in conjunction with the limits on automobile use described later in this chapter.

A small town or a city that wants to have the character of a traditional streetcar suburb might set a maximum height of three stories and also require that the frontage of a development may be no wider than one third of a block. Its commercial streets would have a quaint character, because they would be made up of rows of small buildings, each designed by a different developer. Its neighborhoods might be filled with freestanding houses, row houses, small apartment houses, or some mix of the three, depending on what the market demands. Houses on the same block would have varied designs, because the limit on the size of development means that no more than a few houses could be built at a time. We would avoid the monotony of typical suburban subdivisions.

A city that wants to have the character of a traditional urban neighborhood might set a maximum height of five or six stories and a maximum lot frontage of one-half of a block. With small blocks, this scale could give the neighborhood a character something like Greenwich Village in New York or North Beach in San Francisco: small five or six story buildings with apartments and offices, many of them above shops.

A city that wants to be developed as something more like a mass suburb might set a maximum height limit of three stories and a maximum lot size of one, two, three, or four blocks. This would allow developers to build shopping centers and to mass produce tract-housing, though they would have to design the developments around the small blocks of the street system. This scale of development is small enough that different uses would be developed near each other, and people would be able to walk from their homes to shopping.

(Though we are describing the maximum size in terms of blocks, developers would probably orient their projects to streets, not to blocks. For example, with a maximum development size of two blocks, a developer could build a shopping center on both of the sides of a street that is a major transit route, which would be two blocks long and would take up half of the square block on each side of the street.)

A city that wants to be developed as a local business center might set a maximum height of five or six stories and a maximum lot size of one block. Then it could have large office buildings and apartment buildings, but not the multi-building office complexes that the biggest corporations need.

A city that wants to be a major regional business center might set a maximum height of six stories or twelve stories and a maximum lot size of nine or twelve city blocks, to accommodate large office complexes and housing complexes. Like today's edge-city suburbs, this city would be developed with a mix of shopping centers, office developments, and housing developments, with the mix depending on what the market demands. But this city would be much more walkable than today's edge-city suburbs, because it would be built around a traditional street system.

If a city allows lot sizes as large as nine or twelve blocks, it should probably require that developers provide retail on the outer edges of large developments. There should be a standard that requires a certain amount of retail space for every 1000 square feet of office space or of housing in developments larger than a few blocks. Otherwise, the city could end up with stretches of office parks or of housing developments that have no retail within walking distance. It could also end up with dead zones, like the ones around urban housing projects: if developers build large tracts of just housing, people would have no reason to walk in that direction, and it would hurt businesses on surrounding blocks. Requiring retail on the edges of these large developments would provide local shopping and would give pedestrians a reason to walk in that direction.

Usually, controlling the scale of development does away with the need for this sort of land-use planning: when developments are small, there will be enough diversity that there will be shopping and other services within walking distance of homes and worksites. But when we allow development as large as nine or twelve blocks, we need some planning to require a diversity of land uses.

Realistically, modern metropolitan areas need some large-scale development. We can imagine an ideal world where each building is designed and developed individually and where the economy is so decentralized that large office complexes are not needed. But in the real world, we will need some large-scale tract housing for the foreseeable future, to make housing more affordable. And even if we decentralized the economy as much as possible, we would still have corporations and government agencies that need large office complexes. However, traditional city blocks can accommodate these large developments as well as small developments, as Rockefeller Center proves. Because the city sets a maximum size for development, the large-scale complexes will probably be interspersed with some smaller developments, as Rockefeller Center is, making the city more varied and interesting.

Piecemeal Planning

The early planners clearly were wrong to think that we must rebuild the city in the form of superblocks surrounded by wide arterial streets, in order to accommodate the "great scale" of modern technology. Actually, mass production has not taken over as completely as they expected, and the modern economy has a mixed scale: we have both large and small-scale businesses, shopping districts, and housing developments. Modernist urban design does not work well for the small-scale uses, but traditional neighborhood design can accommodate both the small and large-scale uses.

Even with these large-scale developments, the city will hold together if the street system is laid out first, designed for pedestrians as well as traffic, and large developments are built around the street system. If large housing developments and office complexes are required to fit into the street system, they will be integrated with the rest of the city.

In other words, the city will hold together if it is developed using piecemeal planning, with the street system designed first and both large and small developments added in an ad hoc way.

Of course, there should be a few exceptions to the rule that developers must fit into the street grid. There are some land uses, such as college campuses, that are traditionally designed on a large scale and ignore the street grid. These should be subject to strict design review to insure that they are knit into the surrounding city, rather than turning their backs on their surroundings.

There are also some urban land-uses that have to be kept away from other land uses, such as oil refineries, large factory complexes, and centers of warehousing and distribution. There must be some areas zoned as districts for nuisance industry and for other incompatible uses, and there should be a relatively short list of land uses that are not allowed in the mixed use parts of the city and are required to locate in these industrial zones.

Apart from these exceptions, though, it would be best if cities controlled their character by limiting scale rather than by controlling land use. The modernists wanted to separate functions so each could be designed on a large scale. We should do just the opposite: limit the scale of development so different functions are built within walking distance of each other. If there is an old-fashioned street grid, even large-scale office complexes or housing developments could have shopping and restaurants within easy walking distance.

A metropolitan area could allow different scales in different neighborhoods. If the area were all a single city, it could give its downtown the scale of a major business center, and it could give outlying neighborhoods the scale of streetcar suburbs. But it would be better for the metropolitan area to be divided politically into many smaller cities: this would give citizens more democratic control over the character of local development, and it would have the added advantage of creating juxtapositions of different scales. For example, if one small city that wants to make itself into a regional downtown is near other small cities that want to be developed at the scale of streetcar suburbs, then it will be easy for people who live in these suburbs to get to this small downtown for shopping and other services. In general, the market will generate the local shopping and services that residents demand, and smaller cities have less ability than larger cities to get in the way of this process.

Visual Coherence

For aesthetic and symbolic reasons, height limits should apply only to the ordinary buildings that make up the fabric of the city: housing, shopping, and office buildings. Height limits should not apply to symbolic structures, such as obelisks and bell towers, or to buildings with symbolic importance, such as major government buildings, religious buildings, and schools. In small towns and suburbs, the local churches, high schools, and city halls should stand out above the urban fabric of homes and businesses to establish each neighborhood's identity visually. In cities, the major government buildings, cathedrals, and symbolic structures should stand out above the urban fabric of apartment buildings and office buildings to establish the city's identity visually.

In visual terms, it is best for a city to have a height limit of no more than six stories for fabric buildings. This is the scale that gives visual coherence to traditional European cities, where the cathedral and perhaps the campanile stand out above the urban fabric. We have a similar coherent scale in Washington D.C., where the Capitol dome and Washington Monument stand out above the urban fabric. It is also possible for a city to be visually coherent with a height limit of as much as twelve stories for fabric buildings, if it has symbolic buildings or towers large enough to give it a strong visual identity. With fabric buildings much higher than twelve stories, though, a city is bound to be dominated visually by a crowd of faceless high-rises, like most modern American downtowns; it can still work well as a city, but it will not be visually coherent.

The cathedrals and government buildings that dominate the skylines of traditional cities symbolized the shared values of the people who live there – common religious, cultural and political values. The glass and steel high-rises that dominate the skylines of American cities today symbolize our shared belief in technology and economic growth; the modernists said they were symbols of purely rational decision making, but they look more like symbols of technology that has never been controlled, of a society where growth is not subordinated to human purposes.

If a contemporary American city were built with a six-story height limit for fabric buildings and no limits on symbolically important buildings, it would not center on one religious building, like the cathedral of mediaeval cities whose life centered on a common religion, and it would not center on one or two government buildings, like Washington, DC, a company town where life is dominated by the federal government. It would be much more pluralistic.

In the city center, the largest buildings of the city's major religions would rise above the urban fabric: perhaps a cathedral, a mosque, a Hindu temple. Several different types of civic building would rise above the urban fabric: city hall, the main courthouse, major museums. There might also be a purely symbolic structure in the city center, such as a campanile or a obelisk. Out in the neighborhoods, hundreds of smaller buildings would rise above the urban fabric: church steeples, local library branches, local courthouses, community centers.

These should be designed to make a distinctive mark on the skyline: even if the building proper does not have to be larger than the fabric buildings that surround it, it should include a tower or spire that rises above the fabric. In some cases, we already have conventions that let us identify the type of building from a distance – steeples for churches, minarets for mosques, classical cupolas for government buildings. We should try to create an equally strong visual identity for other types of buildings.

The typical skyline of our cities today is a clutter of faceless high-rises. You cannot even tell by looking at them which are office buildings and which are housing. It is usually boring, because most high-rises look more or less the same, but it is even worse when developers pull in avant-gardist architects who design high-rises that are weird just for the sake of being different. It is usually meaningless, because it is made up of housing and offices, which have no symbolic value, but if one building dominates the skyline, it can create inadvertent symbolism: for example, in downtown Charlotte, North Carolina, the 60-story Bank of America Corporate Center, by the well known modernist architect Cesar Pelli, towers over the usual clutter of faceless high rises, and the skyline very clearly symbolizes the fact that this city is so fixated on growth that the developers can do what they want and the bankers are in charge. (They themselves would say it symbolizes the "economic dynamism" of their city – but that is just another way of saying the same thing.)

The skyline of the city we are imagining would be interesting, with distinctive building types rising above the fabric, including some structures that are unique to the city, like the Duomo of Florence or the Campanile of Venice. This skyline would also be meaningful: the urban fabric represents the necessities of life, housing and business, and the buildings that rise above the fabric represent the things that people believe make their lives worthwhile – religion, culture, self-government.

The city could adopt a law like the informal rule they used to have in Philadelphia saying that no other building in the city could be as high as the statue of William Penn at the top of City Hall. It would be most appropriate for City Hall to rise above all the other buildings. This would symbolize the fact that growth is subject to political control. It would also show that, though the city is diverse and contains a variety of different public buildings, its democratic self-government holds it together.

Limiting Speed

Limits on height and scale are not enough in themselves. Today, if a typical American city limited development to the smallest scale described above, developers could turn its main street into a strip mall, with a fast-food stand surrounded by a parking lot on each site. At other scales, we could have other sorts of auto-oriented development.

We also need limits on automobile use. Even more than limits on scale, these will determine the character of the city and the way of life of its residents.

In this section, we will look at three different limits on the automobile to show the sort of effect that they would have on urban design. We continue our thought experiment by using these three ideal types as models to describe what cities would be like if they were developed from the beginning with a consistent limit on automobile use.

The models all assume that most residents have the typical American preference for neighborhoods of single-family houses. The cities would look very different if the same limits on the automobile were used in Italy, Austria, or other cultures where people prefer higher densities. This assumption is useful because conservatives often claim that Americans want to live in lower density suburbs, and that this would be impossible without giving free rein to the automobile; we will see that the suburbs would work better with limits on the automobile.

Looking at three models, each with a different limit on the automobile applied consistently throughout the entire metropolitan area, is useful as a thought experiment. It will make it clear that, by choosing different sorts of limits on the automobile, we are choosing different ways of life – which is a political decision that people should make for themselves, not a technical decision that should be made by the planners.

A Pedestrian-Oriented City

As the first ideal type, consider a metropolitan area that banned cars and other personal motor vehicles. Residents could still rent cars to use for recreational trips to the country, and motor vehicles would still be used for deliveries and other services. But in-city personal transportation would rely on walking, bicycling, buses, light rail, and commuter rail.

Banning cars and limiting the scale of development could give us a city where most neighborhoods have the density of the streetcar suburbs that were common in American cities a century ago.

Because Americans are wealthier now, virtually everyone who wanted to could live in neighborhoods like the streetcar suburbs where the minority of Americans who were middle class lived before World War I – a time when middle-class Americans did not own vehicles. The streetcar suburbs were a high-point of American urban design. They had private houses on lots that were typically one-tenth of an acre, with small front yards and adequate backyards. There were shopping and trolley lines within easy walking distance of houses, with a few stories of housing above the stores on the main streets. Many stores offered delivery of groceries and heavy goods.

Of course, many people would also want to live in row houses or in apartments, once these higher density neighborhoods were no longer overrun with cars. Nineteenth-century row-house neighborhoods are still very livable for families. Apartments are the most convenient choice for many young people and elderly people.

Compare this model with the cities we have in America today. These streetcar suburbs would be quieter and safer for children than modern suburbia, because the cars would be removed. They would be more neighborly, because people would walk to local shopping and parks and would meet their neighbors along the way. They would be healthier, because of lower air pollution levels and because people would get regular exercise from walking and bicycling: as recently as 1970, more than half of all American children 6 to 11 years old walked to school; today, only 15% of American children walk to school,[111] and obesity has become such a serious problem among children that doctors are calling it an epidemic.

Most people would consider this sort of streetcar suburb a better place to live than modern American suburbia, and it also would be about as convenient in terms of transportation, because of its higher densities and mixed uses. Turn-of-the-century streetcar suburbs had an overall density of about 15 people per acre, while postwar American suburbs had only about 2 people per acre (including, in both cases, the land used for roads, shopping, parking and other uses as well as the land used for housing itself). Streetcar suburbs would save almost seven-eighths of the land eaten up by the sprawl suburbs we build today. The higher density alone would reduce the distance of the average trip by almost two-thirds, but actual trip length would be reduced by more, because smaller-scale development allows more local services – for example, neighborhood shopping rather than regional malls.

It would be possible to provide very frequent transit service in this sort of compact city, where private automobiles do not draw users away from public transit. We would also expect many improvements on the bicycle to appear once people no longer drove cars, such as bicycle trailers to carry small children or cargo, and pedi-cars with light-weight convertible roofs that snap on for rainy days. Even more important, people would not need to use much transportation: it would be quicker to walk to the local store or doctor's office than it is for modern suburbanites to drive to the shopping mall or medical center.

Though it is hard for us to imagine today, one hundred years ago, most middle-class Americans who lived in cities or towns did not own vehicles. Maintaining a carriage was a sign of wealth and was beyond the means of the middle class. Streetcars were used for commuting to work and for occasional trips to other parts of town, and everyone lived within walking distance of a neighborhood shopping street, where you could find stores, doctors' offices, and other everyday services right there in your neighborhood. People nodded to neighbors as they walked to the main street, and they invariably met people they knew at the neighborhood stores.

There is a good picture of the life in middle-class American towns and streetcar suburbs before World War I at the beginning of Booth Tarkington's novel *Seventeen*.[112] The book begins by describing a teenage boy walking home from the soda shop on Central Avenue. At home, he finds that his mother has gotten a bargain by buying some wash tubs at an auction. Because the store that sold them has gone out of business, it will not deliver them; because the tubs must be picked up by the end of the day, there is no time to hire a delivery man; and so the boy has to carry the tubs home. It is only in this sort of extraordinary situation that the family is inconvenienced by not having a vehicle: ordinarily, it is easy to walk to the store, and easy to get bulky goods delivered. The book was written in 1915 – less than a century ago, but it seems like a different world where middle-class American families did not own vehicles, and middle-class teenagers walked to the local main street rather than driving to the mall.

With a ban on automobiles, this ideal type would eliminate the need for land-use planning almost completely – apart from special zoning for noxious industries and other incompatible uses. Commercial uses would tend to be built around transit nodes and transit corridors without any planning, as they were a century ago, because they would have to be located where customers and employees could get to them easily. Some commercial uses would be in neighborhoods as conveniences. Instead of outlawing them through zoning, the city would allow corner stores in neighborhoods: they would be convenient for local residents, they would not attract cars, and they would not turn into boutiques with a regional draw because they are not at transit stops. The city could also allow doctor and dentist offices in neighborhoods, rather than concentrating them all in one regional "pill hill" hospital district. And the city could allow local shopping streets to expand onto nearby side streets if the demand is there: residents would not have to worry about customers driving around their streets looking for parking, because customers would take transit on the main street, and would walk up the side street to get to the shopping.

In addition to eliminating most zoning that specifies land use, this city could also do without urban codes that make sure that buildings are oriented to pedestrians rather than set back behind parking lots. Buildings would be oriented to pedestrians because almost all of their users would be pedestrians. For example, most stores would be built to the sidewalk, as they were in traditional shopping streets, but there would not be the complete uniformity that we have when planners use urban codes; there would also be room for an occasional idiosyncratic variations in the store frontages, such as a setback that allows a restaurant to have more space for seating in front.

A City that Tames the Automobile

As a second ideal type, to illustrate the effect of a different limit on the automobile, consider a city with a speed limit of 12 mph to 15 mph for private vehicles. This limit would let people use cars for local errands, but people would use a higher speed regional rail system for longer trips.

Because of the low speeds, automobiles would no longer dominate transportation and exclude other users. Bicycles and small electric vehicles similar to golf carts could travel along with the automobiles in the main traffic lanes. Shopping streets would be quieter and safer for pedestrians than they are in today's cities. Residential streets could slow traffic even more, as the Woonerfs in the Netherlands do, to make them safe places for children to play.

With this sort of speed limit, there would be a massive shift to public transportation for commuting and for regional shopping. Both office and shopping developments would naturally tend to cluster around transit nodes and corridors, because they would have to locate there, in order to attract customers, clients, and potential employees who use public transit.

With the lower speed, people would travel shorter distances. Because it would take longer to get to regional shopping, for example, most every-day shopping that is now is done in malls would shift to local shopping streets. There would probably be some stores on these local shopping streets where most customers come by car, particularly supermarkets, but most stores would have to appeal to both drivers and pedestrians.

Though densities would not be as high as in Victorian streetcar suburbs, they would be higher than in modern American suburbia. Typically, people might live on one-sixth acre lots – a size midway between the one-tenth acre lots that were common in streetcar suburbs and the one-quarter acre lots of postwar suburbia. Neighborhoods might have the feel of the bungalow neighborhoods that were popular during the 1920s, which had lots about this size.

This city would retain some of the advantages of the car-free streetcar suburb that we looked at earlier, such as good transit services and shopping streets that are relatively near to people's homes, but it would be less neighborly, less compact, noisier, and less safe than the car-free streetcar suburb. It would also have some of the advantages of suburbia: automobiles would let people live in houses with larger lots, haul big loads of groceries to the basement deep-freeze, chauffeur children around the neighborhood, and generally live a more suburban way of life.

This moderate limit on cars would not reduce the need for planning as much as the ban on cars that we looked at earlier. For example, this city would need design guidelines to make sure that parking is located behind stores: many developers would want to put parking in front of the store, to attract drive-by customers, and if they were allowed to do this, it would ruin the street for pedestrians. This city would also would need single-use residential zoning to protect neighborhoods. Neighbors would object to corner stores, because they would draw automobile traffic into the neighborhood. Though it would need some land-use planning, this model would need far less planning to control sprawl and to solve transportation problems than today's cities do.

Suburbia that Works

As a third ideal type, consider a city with an even looser limit on automobile use, an in-city speed limit of 25 or 30 miles per hour.

Even this loose limit on the automobile would do much more to solve our cities' problems than the comprehensive regional land-use and transportation planning that environmentalists usually advocate. Long-distance commuting that is now done by freeway, would shift to public transportation on heavy commuter rail systems. Commercial development would tend to cluster around the rail stations, to take advantage of the regional workforce and customer base that comes by rail: instead of freeway-oriented regional shopping malls, the city would have mixed-use shopping and office complexes (with plenty of parking) at rail stations – though there would also be some districts zoned to accommodate automobile-oriented big-box shopping. Much of the suburban sprawl at the edges of today's metropolitan area would be eliminated because it is totally dependent on high-speed freeway access and would be isolated from jobs and shopping without it.

Yet this speed limit would allow everyone to live a suburban life: if the city had a relatively high-speed commuter rail system, people could all live in suburban neighborhoods in houses with two-car garages on quarter-acre lots.

At this low a density, most people would drive whenever they left their houses, but there would still be major differences from today's suburbia. People who had long commutes would drive to the local train station in order to commute to work. People would generally shop and work in mixed use complexes built around these train stations, with most local customers driving there to do their shopping and with most commuters and regional shoppers coming by rail. Both these differences would both be improvements: commuting by rail is generally less grueling than fighting traffic on the freeway, and mixed-use centers are more interesting and more convenient than shopping malls and office parks.

These changes would cut automobile use at least in half, because most commutes would be shifted from freeway to rail, because most people would drive to nearby shopping, and because workers could walk from their offices to lunch. This reduction in automobile use would dramatically reduce the city's environmental problems.

None of the environmentalists who call for regional governments and massive planning bureaucracies expect as much from them as you could get from a simple political decision to limit automobile speed to 25 or 30 miles per hour.

Because it allows so much automobile use, this city would need a substantial amount of planning. Like the previous model, it would need land-use planning to protect residential neighborhoods from traffic, and it would need urban design guidelines to require businesses to be oriented to pedestrians as well as to cars. Because it allows higher speeds, it would need to plan the street system to protect residential neighborhoods from through traffic: neighborhoods would not be safe or livable if drivers could use them as shortcuts to avoid arterial streets.

Modern suburbia deals with this problem by building housing on cul-de-sacs and twisting streets, but as the New Urbanists have pointed out, this sort of street pattern makes distances so long that is virtually impossible for people to walk from their homes to local services. It is better to use an old-fashioned street grid with traffic diverters, which keep automobile through-traffic off the streets but which do not stop pedestrians and bicyclists. At least the people who live nearest to the shopping streets would walk to them, and some hardy souls would bicycle to them despite the intimidating speed of the traffic.

With all the automobile traffic concentrated on arterial streets, we would also need the planners to do the sort of traffic engineering used in modern American cities to keep traffic flowing – such as left-turn only lanes and signal phases – even though this would make the commercial streets uglier and a bit harder for pedestrians to negotiate.

This model is not at all radical: it is how our cities would have developed after World War Two, if we had retained traditional street patterns, and if we had decided to promote suburbanization by investing in commuter rail systems instead of freeways.

American cities became automobile-oriented without any deliberate decision. People moved from the city to suburbs where they could afford houses, without thinking about the effect they were having on the region as a whole; planners projected and accommodated this trend by building suburban housing and freeways;

and the public never made a deliberate political choice of what sort of cities it would live in. By contrast, this ideal type, with a speed limit of 25 or 30 miles per hour, represents a deliberate, responsible political choice of a suburban way of life: it would let everyone live in suburbia without blighting the entire region with freeways and traffic, and without blighting the earth with global warming.

Outside of the City

Incidentally, regardless of which of these limits is used inside the city, moderate speed limits would also be useful outside of the city.

Building freeways through our countryside turned many of our rural areas into exurbs filled with commuters: for example, much of southern New Hampshire is now essentially a suburb of Boston. Because they were designed by transportation planners whose only goal was to speed traffic, the freeways by-passed small towns: new developments near the freeway interchanges drained business from nearby Main Streets. The freeways also fragmented the open countryside and reduced wildlife populations.

Outside of cities, our goal should be to replace the freeways with old-fashioned country roads designed for speeds of 45 miles per hour or so. Rather than bypassing towns, these country roads should go through the towns' Main Streets, where they should be slowed to the speed of local traffic. By slowing traffic in this way, we would shift many long-distance automobile trips and most freight hauling to rail: there are abandoned and semi-abandoned tracks all over the country that could be upgraded relatively inexpensively, without the cost of purchasing new rights of way.

Small towns that have been neglected during the last fifty years would revive, once they had a railway station in the center of town and cars driving through slowly on Main Street again, as they did during the early twentieth century.

Rural roads would be used primarily by local people and by people driving for pleasure; people in a hurry would take rail. The people who drove would actually get a feel for the countryside and the towns they passed through, rather that driving on a freeways that feel the same everywhere.

Today, for example, when Californians go skiing in Utah, they fly to Salt Lake City and then rent a car at the airport to drive to the ski resort, but when Californians go skiing in the Sierras, they drive across the state on freeways to the ski resort. If there were country roads with lower speeds, people who wanted a slow, leisurely trip would still drive across the state to go skiing in the Sierras; it would take longer and be more pleasurable than the drive is today. People in a hurry would take the train to the Sierras and rent a car at the station to drive to the ski resort. With high-speed rail, it would be faster to go by train than it now is to drive, and the central valley and the Sierras would not be as overwhelmed with automobiles as they are today.

Political Limits or Planning

As a thought experiment, we have compared three ideal types of cities that consistently apply different limits on the automobile – a ban on automobiles, a 12 or 15 mile per hour speed limit, and a 25 or 30 mile per hour speed limit. This thought experiment lets us compare the two different approaches to controlling urban growth: the direct political limits on growth described in this chapter and our usual method of controlling growth through planning. It shows that direct political limits on growth are more effective than planning, are more democratic than planning, and allow more freedom of choice than planning.

More Effective

We can see that political limits on growth are more effective than planning by comparing our three models with Portland, Oregon, which has the most effective and most environmentally oriented regional land-use and transportation planning in the United States. As we have seen, Portland's urban growth boundary and its zoning to concentrate new development in downtown and in pedestrian- and transit-oriented neighborhoods were projected to reduce per capita automobile use by less than 11% in five decades. Automobile use is reduced relatively slowly, because even with strict zoning to concentrate new development around transit, most people still live in older auto-oriented neighborhoods, and most people still drive to distant shopping centers and jobs. Even its relatively small reduction in automobile use is possible only because Portland has also made political decisions to limit automobile use, for example, by removing the Harbor Drive freeway, and by converting two downtown streets into transit malls. Without the political will to occasionally put this sort of direct limit on the automobile, the planning would have reduced auto use even less.

By contrast, if we had the political will to limit the speed of automobiles, we could do much more than Portland has done with all its planning. For example, reducing automobile speeds by 10% or 20%, could reduce traffic overnight as much as Portland's planning will in five decades, because lower speeds would encourage local shopping and shorter commutes by everyone, not just by those who live in the new neighborhoods around transit.

More Democratic

Political limits on urban growth also are more democratic than planning, because limits on scale and speed are issues that ordinary people can understand and vote on, while regional planning is so complicated that most people cannot fully understand the technical issues involved and do not have the time that it takes to participate in the planning process. Most people resist proposals for regional land use planning for exactly this reason: they know they can have some influence over the local zoning board but that they could have no influence at all over a remote regional planning agency.

Our three models show that, underlying the technical questions that land-use and transportation planners deal with, there are political questions that should be decided democratically – questions about the sort of life that people want to live. A ban on automobiles would create pedestrian-oriented neighborhoods, a 30 mile per hour speed limit would create suburbia, and these different neighborhood designs obviously involve different ways of life.

The ban on automobiles limits private satisfactions for the sake of the public realm, with people foregoing cars to live in neighborhoods that are quieter, safer, and more neighborly.

The 30 mile per hour speed limit sacrifices these public goods for the sake of private satisfactions, with people living on larger lots and having two cars per family.

This is a decision about how we want to live, so it is a decision that ordinary people should make for themselves. It is not a technical decision that should be made by experts in urban planning.

Planning is inherently undemocratic, because planners make decisions by correlating and analyzing information that is not accessible to people who are not specially trained experts. By contrast, the idea that we need political limits on technology means that building a livable city requires political decisions that ordinary people can make democratically.

More Freedom of Choice

Political limits on urban growth also allow more individual freedom of choice than planning. After a city made the initial political choice to adopt the limit on automobile use in one of our three models, the mix of single-family houses, row houses, and apartment buildings in the city would depend on individuals' decisions about how they want to live.

When we discussed these three models, we assumed that most people would have the usual American preference for low density: even with a total ban on cars, they would move to streetcar suburbs, as Americans did a century ago. But if people preferred more urban neighborhoods, any of these three limits on automobile use would lead to a higher density city. Instead of the density of a streetcar suburb, the first model could give us the density of a traditional European city – but without the cars – if people chose to live at that sort of urban density.

The final shape of the city would depend on individuals' choices about what sort of neighborhoods they want to live in, as well as on the political choice about limiting the automobile. With the same limit on the automobile, cities would turn out differently in places where people put a premium on privacy and green space (as they historically have in America and England) and in places where people prefer urban neighborhoods (as they historically have in Italy or Austria).

Comprehensive regional planning restricts individual's choice of the type of housing they can live in: the mix of different housing types and densities is a technical decision, made by experts who run the computer models that analyze the region's land use and transportation system. By contrast, with political limits on technology, the type of housing that is built would depend on people's individual choices. In any of these three models, people could choose to live at higher or lower densities; transportation planners would have to project these trends and provide the public transportation needed to accommodate them.

More Livable

Finally, these three models show that we must limit automobile use to make our cities more livable. Any of the three models works better, is more attractive, and is more livable than modern, freeway-oriented suburbia.

The idea that we can make transportation work better by limiting transportation is counterintuitive. If people are stuck in traffic jams on the freeways, their gut response is that we need wider freeways and maybe also rail systems to get some people off the freeways – and that limiting speeds would make it even harder for them to get around.

In fact, the distance that the average American drives doubles every few decades.[113] Are Americans better off today than we were in the 1960s because we drive twice as much as we did then?

We travel more precisely because we have built so many freeways and other forms of high-speed transportation. Research has shown that people have a roughly constant amount of time that they budget to transportation: if they can travel at higher speeds, they travel longer distances rather than spending less time traveling.

The idea that there is a constant amount of time budgeted for transportation, so that higher speeds just make people travel longer distances, was first advanced by Yacov Zahavi of the U.S. Department of Transportation, who studied changes in travel patterns between 1958 and 1970 and found that people did not spend any less time traveling, at a time when massive freeway construction let them travel much faster.[114]

Follow-up research confirmed his conclusions. It showed that the amount of time that Americans spend commuting to work has remained constant since the 1840s, when the movement to the suburbs began as a reaction against the industrial revolution, despite the vast changes in technology since then.[115] The total amount of time that Americans budget to transportation also tends to remain constant, about 1.1 hours per day.[116]

As speeds have increased, the suburbs have sprawled over more land, the malls and big-box stores have attracted customers from further away, and the distances we drive have gotten longer.

Regardless of the limit we put on transportation, people would spend about the same time traveling. When we decide what limit to put on transportation, the question that we should ask is what sort of city we want to live in. Higher speeds do not save people time, but they do allow people to live in different types of neighborhoods.

Any of the limits on transportation that we have looked at would reduce the need for planning. Some planning would still be needed, of course: even with a total ban on automobiles, transportation planners would still have to lay out streets and transit lines by projecting future residential patterns and future demand for transportation, and we would still need planning to run large park systems, to reserve areas for nuisance industries, and so on. With less stringent limits on automobiles, we would need even more planning, including zoning. But even with the least stringent limit we looked at, a 30 mile per hour speed limit, it would be much less difficult than it is today to provide efficient transportation, to control sprawl, to control pollution, to build viable city centers, and to protect the region's open space. Any of these political limits on urban growth would eliminate many of our cities' environmental problems and make it easier for the planners to solve the remaining problems. And any of these limits would also dramatically reduce larger environmental problems, such as global warming.

Our models are ideal types with the same limit on transportation imposed throughout the metropolitan area, but in practice, political limits on the automobile do not have to be consistent throughout a metropolitan region. Local municipalities could make their own decisions to lower speeds; large cities could lower speeds or ban cars only in certain areas, as many European cities have banned cars in parts of the city center. Any local decisions to limit the automobile would reduce the transportation problems and the environmental problems of the entire region.

Chapter 6
The Next Steps

Technocratic planners have always said that we should replace the irrational patchwork of city governments with a regional land-use and transportation planning authority, which could deal with all of the region's problems in a comprehensive way. The old political divisions should be replaced with a single regional planning authority, because in modern societies, political decisions are not as important as the technical tasks of planning.

In reality, to reclaim our cities, we need to do almost the opposite: we need to recover the *political* use of government, so we can use the law to limit technology. We do need some special-purpose regional planning agencies that cut across local jurisdictions and are responsible for transportation, for air and water pollution control, and the like, but we do not need centralized control of all regional land-use and transportation planning. Instead, we need to begin making responsible political decisions to limit technology, in order to cut our cities' problems down to a size that the planners have some chance of solving.

The three models in the previous chapter showed that urban planning should be subordinate to political choice. In this chapter, we will look at the practical political actions that are needed as the next steps to rebuilding our cities.

Stopping Freeways

The political struggle for our cities began with the anti-freeway movement of the 1960s. During the 1950s and 1960s, there were plans to cut freeways through the hearts of most major American cities. For example, Robert Moses wanted to build three cross-Manhattan freeways that would have destroyed the city's pedestrian feel. In San Francisco, planners wanted to slice up the city's neighborhoods and hide its waterfront with freeways, but in 1961, San Francisco residents stopped the Embarcadero freeway, which would have cut the city off from the waterfront: freeway construction had already begun, and beyond the last off-ramp, there was a freeway stub hanging in the air for decades, showing where the freeway was supposed to continue. After beginning in San Francisco, the anti-freeway movement spread across the country, and by the end of the 1970s, it was virtually impossible to build new freeways in the centers of most major cities, though freeways continue to be built at the urban fringes.

An essential first step in reclaiming our cities and our countryside is to stop building freeways. Funding is needed to maintain existing roads and freeways. New freeways may be needed under unusual circumstances, but the freeway planners should be required to prove that some special circumstance makes it necessary before adding new freeway capacity. Apart from that, all the funding that now goes to expanding freeway capacity should go to public transportation, to bicycling, and to improvements for pedestrians.

In 1991, there was a small shift away from the federal government's pro-freeway bias with the passage of the Intermodal Surface Transportation Efficiency Act (ISTEA), which replaced the old Highway Trust Fund, dedicated solely to freeway construction, with funding for multi-modal transportation. ISTEA and its successor laws were a step in the right direction, but most of the funding still goes to freeways.[117] Freeways are still being built in the countryside and on the edges of metropolitan areas, where they do the most to encourage sprawl. In some cases, citizens' groups make heroic efforts to stop them: In Indiana, Citizens for Appropriate Rural Roads has been working against the Dept. of Transportation for many years to stop the I-69 freeway, which would cut through some of the state's best farming land. But when exurban or rural freeways are proposed, there usually are not enough people around to stop them, as there are in the city, and the planners in the state departments of transportation build the freeways without many citizens thinking about them.

The transportation planners are still at it even in Great Britain, where the anti-freeway movement is much stronger than in the United States.

During the 1980s, the Thatcher Administration developed plans to build freeways throughout the country in order to encourage the development of American-style shopping centers on the edges of towns: to emphasize how much it would do to spur investment and economic growth, they called the plan "Roads to Prosperity." There was a huge public outcry against this plan, which cut across the usual political boundaries. It was opposed by staid Tory ladies who wanted to preserve the traditional character of England, and by self-styled anarchists who protested freeway plans by illegally sitting in trees on the proposed routes. There was such strong opposition to the Thatcher plan that three-quarters of the funding for the National Roads Programme was eliminated within five years, and even the construction industry realized that it has lost the battle over new roads.[118] Ultimately, virtually all of the proposed new roads were stopped. The UK changed its planning policies to make it more difficult to build freeways: highway planners must base their planning on the assumption that providing capacity can induce enough demand to fill that capacity.[119] The opposition to freeways was so successful that Alarm-UK, the umbrella group coordinating all the anti-freeway protests, dissolved itself on the grounds that it was no longer needed.

But after a lull, the UK's transportation planners came up with a new plan for building more freeways. In 2000, the government released a transportation plan that had a relatively strong environmental bias: more of its £121 billion funding went to public transportation than to roads, and much of the road funding was for maintenance. Yet the plan did include an explicit target of widening 5% of the country's roads and building thirty new bypasses around towns,[120] though much of England's anti-freeway activism focused on stopping bypasses, because they pave the open countryside and drain life out of towns. The planners tried to take a balanced approach – but, after all, they are transportation planners whose job is to provide people with mobility, and sometimes they will find that building roads is the way to provide mobility.

The best model of citizen activism is in Switzerland, where voters passed an initiative in 1994 to ban all freeway expansion, despite opposition from their own government and from the European Community's transportation experts. Switzerland also has a law banning all trucks over 28 tons, to reduce the environmental effect of truck traffic and to shift freight onto rail.[121] These direct political actions to limit environmentally destructive forms of transportation give us much better results than we would gotten if the Swiss had considered these issues technical problem in transportation planning and placed them in the hands of a regional planning authority. Yet these political actions would have been impossible if Switzerland had joined the European Community and surrendered some of its sovereignty to the continent's transportation planners.

Controlling Sprawl

Along with the political battles to stop freeways and slow traffic, there have been many political battles during recent decades to stop suburban sprawl and out-of-scale development.

Wal-Marts and other superstores have sometimes been stopped in rural parts of the country – most notably in Vermont – where they threaten the character of its small towns. We also need to stop freeway-oriented superstores in cities, where they threaten neighborhood shopping streets. Big-box discount stores, such as Costco and the Price Club, are now driving older supermarkets out of business, just as supermarkets drove independent grocers and corner stores out of business a half-century ago. Neighborhood supermarkets that have been in business for decades are closing, no longer economically viable once they have lost 10 or 15% of their business to larger superstores a few freeway exits away. People in these neighborhoods who do not have cars suddenly find it difficult to buy food.

Britain implemented national planning guidelines that strictly limit suburban shopping centers after a government survey found that one new shopping center, with parking for 10,000 cars, took

70% of its shoppers from the nearest town and many shoppers from other surrounding towns.[122] We need similar legislation in the United States.

There have also been many successful political battles to stop low-density, automobile-dependent suburban housing development. The Sierra Club alone has stopped hundreds of developments all over the country that would have suburbanized open space. During the last decade, a number of states have developed more general policies to stop sprawl. As we have seen, Oregon requires all cities to establish an Urban Growth Boundary (UGB), a line beyond which suburban development is not allowed. Maryland concentrates state investments in infrastructure in existing cities and towns and does not subsidize infrastructure for new sprawl development. Other states should adopt similar policies to stop sprawl.

Zoning Choice

The most important thing we can do to stop sprawl is simply to loosen up local zoning laws that require sprawl. Despite the talk about smart growth, municipalities and counties all over the country still have zoning laws based on the 1950s ideal of suburbia, which require developers to build low-density, single-use projects. All this land-use planning is the greatest contributor to sprawl today, as it was in the 1950s.

We have seen that the New Urbanists have begun building more traditional neighborhoods, which are popular with home buyers, but developers who want to build in this style almost always must go through a burdensome process to get around the standard zoning. Most developers are not willing to spend the extra time and money needed to get zoning variances, so they build the conventional suburban development required by the zoning laws.

The National Association of Governors has estimated that about one-third of Americans would prefer to live in traditional neighborhood developments, but that only 1% of the new housing available is in this type of neighborhood, because zoning laws all over the country require developers to build low-density, single-use suburbia. The Congress for the New Urbanism has estimated that, in the next decade, because of demographic changes and continuing changes in taste, 55% of all American homebuyers would prefer to live in traditional neighborhoods if they had the choice.[123]

A number of cities across the country have given people this choice by adopting Traditional Neighborhood Development (TND) zoning laws in parallel with their conventional zoning laws: developers can choose to use either of the two zoning standards. In 1999, Wisconsin passed a state law requiring all cities and towns with more than 12,500 people to adopt TND zoning laws, which can either be the sole code regulating development or can be used in parallel with their conventional zoning laws, giving developers the choice of which they want to follow.

Other states should do the same as Wisconsin, by requiring cities to allow zoning choice. We know more about the problems that conventional suburban zoning causes today than we did in the 1950s. We should realize by now that it is foolish to legislate sprawl.

Current laws that allow zoning choice generally apply only to larger greenfield developments, but zoning choice is also needed in existing suburbs, to allow developers to rebuild shopping centers and strip malls as pedestrian oriented neighborhoods. New Urbanists have begun to do this all over the country.[124] One of the first examples was Andres Duany's Mashpee Commons,[125] which converted a 1950s shopping mall in Cape Cod into a development that looks like a traditional town center, and Duany found that the main obstacle to building this project was zoning: for example, the zoning laws required setbacks that made it illegal to build storefronts facing the sidewalk, and in order to get around the law, Duany had to say that the streets of this traditional development were the internal circulation system of a shopping mall.

The movement to rebuild malls and strip malls would spread through the country and change the character of suburbia, if only we changed the zoning laws so it was not illegal. We cannot allow zoning choice in the residential neighborhoods of existing suburbs. It would not be politically feasible to pass laws that let developers demolish two houses on an existing suburban street and replace them with five houses. In fact, we would not want these extra houses added to a residential suburb, where the street system makes walking impossible.

But if we allowed zoning choice for commercially zoned areas in existing suburbs, it would change their character by giving them walkable centers, and it would raise their density enough to support better public transportation.

The smart growth movement has had many successes, but it would be much more successful if it changed its tactics in one important way: it should start lobbying for zoning choice instead of for comprehensive regional planning.

Zoning choice has important political advantages over the usual demands for comprehensive regional planning. Conservatives attack regional planning by saying that people prefer living in suburbia and that environmentalists are trying to use big government to force people to live in a way that they do not want to live. Ordinary people are suspicious of regional planning because it takes power from local government and restricts individual choice by letting planners decide what types of housing will be available.

Proposals for zoning choice sidestep the usual conservative criticism of environmentalists by making it clear that sprawl is not the result of free consumer choice. Sprawl is caused by government planning, by zoning laws that force developers to follow the 1950s suburban ideal. Conservatives cannot very well attack zoning choice by saying that people should be forced to live in sprawl, even if they do not want to. If the environmental movement began to emphasize zoning choice, traditional neighborhood development would sweep across the country, because no one can argue against giving people this choice.

Zoning choice is such an obvious winner that it is hard to understand why environmentalists have not made it one of the key policies that they advocate politically. There is only one explanation: they are so used to demanding top-down solutions imposed by the planners that they cannot imagine giving people more choice.

Controlling Speed

Finally, we also need to slow automobile traffic. There are three possible ways of doing this: limiting speeds on neighborhood streets, removing automobile lanes on arterial streets, and reducing speeds on freeways.

Limiting Speed on Neighborhood Streets

We have to limit speeds on local streets to make walkable neighborhoods safe enough that people with children want to live in them rather than in suburban cul-de-sacs. To keep walkable neighborhoods safe and livable, existing neighborhoods need "traffic calming" to limit speeds, and new neighborhoods need streets designed for lower speeds.

Many European cities have calmed traffic dramatically. In the Netherlands and Germany, many residential streets have been converted to *Woonerfs*, redesigned to slow traffic to five or ten miles per hour.

Traffic calming on residential streets has also begun in the United States, generally using simple and inexpensive methods such as speed humps, gradual undulations in the road that make it uncomfortable to drive more than 15 miles per hour. The city of Oakland, CA, planned to begin a study to determine the best way to protect residential streets from high-speed traffic, but there was such strong neighborhood pressure for immediate action that the city decided to install speed humps in five hundred locations before even beginning the study. Many cities have also used more expensive devices to slow traffic, such as islands in the center of roads or roundabouts at intersections.

The New Urbanists design new neighborhoods with streets that work for pedestrians as well as for cars, by making streets and lanes narrower and making turning radii tighter. New Urbanism has begun to influence official design standards for new roads. Research has shown that the usual standards for street design, which require wide lanes, wide shoulders, and straight roads, encourage people to travel above the speed limit. The Institute of Transportation Engineers (ITE) issued alternative street-design guidelines in 1998, which allow narrower streets in urban neighborhoods, and narrower, curving roads in the country, to slow traffic.[126] The ITE represents more progressive traffic engineers, but we can expect this movement to spread to more conventional traffic engineers in coming decades.

Removing Traffic Lanes on Arterial Streets

There has also been some movement in American cities and suburbs to remove traffic lanes on arterial streets, slowing traffic.

American cities are beginning to give transit priority over cars by converting lanes from general use to transit lanes, which not only speeds up transit but also slows cars by reducing the road capacity available to them. Cities have also begun to use technology that allows transit drivers to preempt traffic lights with electronic devices that turn the light green as the bus approaches: lights on these streets are currently timed to optimize the flow of automobile traffic, so that these devices slow down automobile traffic as well as speeding up transit.

Some American suburbs have begun to convert strip malls into urban boulevards with slower traffic. One well known example is Walter Kulash's redesign of the main street of Winter Park, Florida, near Orlando, where he was the city's traffic engineer. Before he started, the street was a typical strip mall, with three lanes of high-speed traffic in each direction, no on-street parking, and parking lots facing the sidewalk. Kulash converted this strip into an old-fashioned Main Street, by replacing two traffic lanes with curbside parking, by planting street trees, and by changing the zoning so developers had to build new stores facing the sidewalk, with parking behind them. The on-street parking slows traffic, because cars have to stop when someone is parallel parking. Storefronts on the sidewalk also slow traffic, because they make the scene interesting enough that people want to slow down to see it. These changes reduced the average speed on the street to 15 miles per hour, and they also made it a very successful shopping street. Kulash points out that many people driving though do not have to be there at all; they choose to drive there because they enjoy being on the street.[127]

Because he was so successful in Winter Park, Kulash is now in demand as a consultant, using similar methods to revitalize declining downtowns in older cities around the country.[128] Some suburbs are beginning to get the idea by adding on-street parking and pedestrian oriented uses to their strip malls, as the New Urbanists suggest.

Reducing Freeway Speeds

Reducing speed limits on freeways is one of the most effective things we can do to reduce traffic regionally, but of course, it would also be one of the most controversial.

In one experiment, eleven of Switzerland's twenty-six cantons reduced the speed limit on all highways to 80 kilometers per hour (about 50 miles per hour) for five days in February, 2006, in an attempt to reduce high levels of air pollution caused by fine particulates. They found that overall traffic on the highways decreased by 14%, and that traffic flowed more smoothly with no traffic jams. Particulate emissions near highways went down by 5% to 10% but went back up after the experiment ended.[129]

Consider how much more effective reducing speed is than regional planning. Switzerland cut traffic by 14% overnight by reducing speed. Portland expects to cut traffic by 11% in fifty years using regional planning.

A number of American cities have slowed traffic dramatically by removing freeways and replacing them with surface streets, The trend began on the west coast, in the environmentally conscious cities where we would expect this sort of experimental project: Portland removed Harbor Drive in the 1970s, and San Francisco removed the Embarcadero Freeway and Central Freeway during the 1990s. The trend moved to the American heartland when Milwaukee, Wisconsin, removed the Park East freeway and replaced it with a street grid. Eight other American cities have adopted plans to remove freeways.[130] However, these cities are generally removing minor freeway spurs that blight central neighborhoods in order to promote economic development, and they generally consider the slower traffic an undesirable side-effect of the plan.

In Seattle, the Alaska Way Viaduct, a major freeway that cuts the city off from its waterfront, has reached the end of its life, and there is a strong citizen's movement to remove it and replace it with surface streets and transit. Citizens voted in a referendum to reject plans to replace it with a new elevated or underground freeway. Mayor Greg Nickels continued to push a plan to build an underground replacement freeway. As a result, he was voted out in November 2009, beaten by Sierra Club activist Mike McGinn, who made his name by fighting against this freeway.

Though the movement to slow freeway traffic is currently an uphill battle, it is conceivable that more people will begin to support this movement, if we recognize that building livable cities requires this sort of political choice. In Seattle, the political movement to remove the Alaska Way and replace it with a slower surface boulevard will transform the region if it succeeds, and this could spur similar changes elsewhere.

Limits on Parking

Apart from reducing speeds, other limits on the automobile are also useful. For example, most cities now set minimum parking requirements for new development that are high enough to accommodate all the automobiles that are projected to come if free parking is provided. These requirements are a self-fulfilling prophesy: because the free parking is provided, the cars come.

Instead, cities could set a maximum parking limit for new developments – perhaps 2 or 2.5 spaces per 1000 square feet for shopping, about half the usual suburban standard. This standard is low enough that it would encourage developers to locate stores where they attract customers who come by walking and by transit. It would also prevent developers from building shopping centers out in the countryside and drawing customers out of the city by providing unlimited free parking.

With this standard in place, businesses would have to charge for parking to ration the available spaces, giving people an incentive to use other forms of transportation. Like limits on speed, this limit on parking requires a responsible political decision that may cause a bit of inconvenience in the short run but that will make the city more livable in the long run.

Transforming our Cities

If we shifted funds from freeway expansion to public transportation and pedestrian safety, if we allowed zoning choice, and if we began to lower speeds and limit parking, we could transform

American cities as dramatically in the next few decades as they were transformed during the postwar decades.

Freeways are perennially congested because of induced demand, and suburbanization can continue only because we are constantly increasing freeway capacity. If we stopped expanding the freeway system and we provided high-quality public transit on exclusive rights of way, people would flock to transit-oriented neighborhoods because of their convenience. Older neighborhoods would attract new infill development, because they were originally built around public transportation and would be the prime beneficiaries of revived transit. Most new development would also be transit-oriented, because it would be the most convenient way for people to get around.

Ultimately, the goal would be to go further and move gradually toward something like the three models described in the previous chapter. So far, freeways have only been torn down in the center of cities, where there are obviously better uses for the land. After a few decades of expanded public transportation and transit-oriented development, it may become possible to begin transforming entire metropolitan areas to make them transit-oriented rather than freeway-oriented.

This seems like a radical change, but fossil fuel depletion and global warming may provide the impetus that lets us make radical changes during this century.

And after all, the changes our cities need during the twenty-first century are less radical than the changes that occurred during the twentieth century. If we followed the most extreme model described in the previous chapter and banned cars entirely, that would undo the changes that happened during the last century and bring back the sort of neighborhood where the American middle class lived in 1900. But no one would predict such an extreme change: some neighborhoods may ban cars, but some neighborhoods undoubtedly will continue to allow them. The changes in our cities that the most radical environmentalists hope for during the twenty-first century are not as extreme as the change from pedestrian and transit-oriented cities to completely automobile-dependent cities that hard-headed traffic engineers and suburban zoners brought us during the twentieth century.

Chapter 7
The End of Modernism

No one today believes in the complete technological determinism of the technocrats and the early city planning theorists. Events have overtaken this view: the environmental movement has stopped many dams, freeways, and power projects by showing that they would damage the quality of life, so it is no longer possible to claim, as Jacques Ellul did, that choice of technology is no more feasible than "personal choice, in respect to magnitude, between 3 and 4."[131]

Yet a vestige of technological determinism lives on in the widespread belief that the problems of modern society involve such complex issues that decisions about how we live must be made by planners on technical grounds. This book has shown that individual and political choice of technology is possible, that we can put the planners in their place if we think about the city in human terms. When we think about what a city's design means in terms of how we live, then we can choose technology on human grounds.

The early planners believed we needed city planning to accommodate modernization and growth. Today, we should be able to see that we must set political limits on destructive forms of modernization and growth – and that these limits will reduce the need for city planning.

Modernism in Its Dotage

In both architecture and city planning, the old modernist doctrines have been discredited.

In architecture, modernism is moribund, but it is dying a slow death. The functionalist architecture of the early and mid twentieth century was modernism in its prime – vigorous, filled with a sense of its moral superiority, out to change the world – but today's avant gardist architecture is modernism in its dotage. The modernist establishment still has power: avant gardists like Frank Gehry and Daniel Libeskind get the commissions for museums and for other buildings that are self-consciously artistic, and avant gardists regularly win the Pritzker Prize, which bills itself as the Nobel Prize for architecture. But this establishment modernism has lost its social content. No one today believes in the functionalists' theories about "honest" design or about technocracy bringing us a better world.

Modernist architecture is in the position that academic art was in during the late nineteenth century: it still has the support of the establishment, but it is just an echo of a style that has not had real vitality for at least a generation.

In urban design, the shift away from modernism has gone even further than in architecture: modernism is completely dead as both a social and an esthetic ideal. Developers still churn out modernist projects where the zoning laws require them, but innovative urban designers and writers about urban design all have rejected modernism, and all are trying to rebuild the traditional urbanism that was destroyed by modernism.

Modernism began as a radical movement, but now it is the status quo. Early in the twentieth century, socialists and other radicals believed modernist architecture was the style that would lead us to the ideal planned society of the future, but no one today believes that Frank Gehry, Daniel Libeskind and other belated modernists are leading us toward a better society. Today, the political idealists are the environmentalists and preservationists who fight to stop modernist projects. The New Urbanists are the ones who believe that they are leading us toward a better society, that their neo-traditional designs will produce cities that are more environmentally sustainable and that have a stronger sense of community than modern cities.

Unfortunately, some New Urbanists have been apologetic about not using modernist architecture, explaining that they use neo-traditional architecture only because the market demands it and that their urban codes can also accommodate modernist buildings. They should be able to see that the modernist symbolism is wrong. Modernist architecture, in its prime, expressed the idea that we should scrap the past entirely and rebuild a purely rational modern world, but we should know by now that is wiser to modernize selectively. In some cases, modern technology is obviously an improvement: when we buy old houses, we want to remodel them by giving them modern heating systems, bathrooms, and kitchens; we do not want them to have coal-burning heaters and stoves, as they did a century ago. But it does not follow that we should scrap every traditional element of design and build houses that are shiny boxes of concrete, steel, and glass.

Technical Questions and Human Questions

We need to reject the modernists' technological determinism by seeing that decisions about design involve human questions as well as technical questions. We must decide what to design as well as how to design it.

If we do not want a freeway to collapse, we must let the engineers design it on the basis of their technical knowledge; but we are wrong to reduce the question of whether the freeway should be built at all to a technical decision that transportation planners make on the basis of projected traffic volumes and cost-benefit studies. Engineers and planners have no special competence to decide whether our cities should be built around the automobile, because this is a decision about how we want to live.

When we think about the human purposes of technological decisions, we can put the planners in their proper place. The traditional relationship between an architect and a client is a good example of the way that ordinary people should control experts. Architects have special knowledge about materials, structures, and other technical questions, which let them make certain decisions about designing a house, but the clients know how they want to live, which lets them make the fundamental decisions about what sort of house the architect should design for them to live in.[132]

Ordinary people should have similar power over fundamental decisions about urban design, so they can decide what sort of cities and neighborhoods they want to live in.

Decentralizing

Decentralizing government could give ordinary people some control over some decisions that are now made by planners.

The conventional wisdom says we should replace local zoning boards, which the average person can try to influence politically, with comprehensive regional land use and transportation planning agencies, which are so remote and deal with such complex technical issues that they leave the average person helpless. Ideally, we should do just the opposite: we should decentralize local government as much as possible, to give people more control over how their own neighborhoods are designed and to create a stronger sense of community.

Though we will never get back to the New England town meeting, there are many decisions that can still be made locally. The San Francisco Bay Area developed in a more decentralized way than other American cities, and it still has many small municipalities near its core, including a few with populations of only 10,000 to 20,000. There are larger special districts to provide water, regional parks, public transportation, and the like, but these small cities have their own zoning departments, their own park departments, their own police departments, their own traffic engineering departments with authority over their streets (except for a few major streets that have been designated as state highways), and their own City Councils that pass all the usual municipal legislation. They are no less efficient than larger cities in the region, and they are certainly much more efficient than large cities such as New York and Los Angeles.

Ideally, we should break up our cities into small self-governing municipalities like these. When a city's population is greater than 100,000, it becomes difficult for the average person to deal with the bureaucracy or to get anything done politically, but in cities of 20,000 or 30,000, people can have a voice in deciding how their own streets and neighborhood parks can be improved. Regional planners must lay out transit lines, major arterial roads, and regional parks, but small municipalities can do the best job of designing local streets, parks and plazas. Small municipalities can also take the lead on larger political issues: for example, small cities have been among the first to pass laws banning styrofoam containers, promoting recycling and illegalizing discrimination against the handicapped. Decentralized city governments can give ordinary people a say on this sort of major national issue.[133]

If it is not politically possible to break up a large city, it may still be possible to decentralize its planning. A large city could be divided into planning districts of, say 50,000 people each, which have their own zoning departments, traffic engineers, parks departments, and planning commissions. It is important that there not only be a local planning commission but also a decentralized planning bureaucracy that is responsible to the local commission. When local planning boards deal with city-wide traffic engineering, zoning, and parks departments, they have to make immense efforts to get the mayor to control the city bureaucracy, and they have very little power of their own. Of course, the city or region as a whole needs its own traffic engineering and park department to deal with major roads and large parks, but the planning districts also need their own traffic engineering and park departments to deal with local streets and parks.

Decentralization would let people take a first step toward political responsibility: after they have acted locally as citizens, they would be more likely to act regionally and nationally as citizens. Decentralization would also help create local community as people dealt with their neighbors politically – though this would often be a conflictful community.

Yet decentralization cannot work in cities built as modern automobile oriented developments. Decades ago, for example, a new high-rise housing project was built next to the freeway in the smallest of the cities in the center of the Bay Area, raising its population from 4,500 to 6,000 people. When the project was done, local political activists discovered that the project's security system would not let them in, so they suddenly could not leaflet about one-quarter of the city's voters. And they also could not leaflet the new residents on the city's streets, because people living in this development usually drove right to the freeway whenever they left their apartments. Most of these new residents know more about what is happening in Washington or New York, which are heavily covered on television, than they do about what is happening in their own city, because they live at the scale of the freeway rather than living in their own city. People must walk around their neighborhoods before they can govern their own neighborhoods.

Thinking Qualitatively

Though decentralization is useful for promoting democratic self-government, there are obviously many decisions in a modern society that must be made centrally, such as decisions about designing the regional transportation system. Even though they cannot be decentralized, these decisions can still be controlled democratically if people think about them concretely and qualitatively.

This change in the way we think about technological decisions is far more important than decentralizing decision making. Decentralization can let people control details of local design. But this book has shown that people can use the law to control the big decisions about technology if we think about these decisions in concrete human terms, as decisions about how we live our lives, rather than being mystified by the planners' abstractions. We need to move beyond the planners' quantitative studies and to think about these decisions qualitatively.

As long as we think that abstractions such as transportation, housing, and pollution control are our "urban problems," we will let city planners and other experts decide what kinds of neighborhoods we live in. For example, one set of planners will analyze the "transportation problem" quantitatively and come up with a solution that moves people efficiently – and people will not see that this decision controls the way that they live.

By contrast, when we think about cities qualitatively, in human terms – as we did when we looked at the three ideal types described in Chapter 5 – it becomes obvious that people should make the political and personal choices that control the city's design. Traffic engineers and city planners are the experts on "solving the transportation problem," but ordinary people are the experts on what sort of city they want to live in.

As we saw in Chapter 5, different political limits on technology create cities with different ways of life. A 30 mile per hour speed limit would promote suburbia and a way of life that focuses on private satisfactions, such as houses on large lots and two cars for each family. A ban on automobiles would promote a way of life that focuses on public goods rather than on private satisfactions: people would live on smaller lots and without automobiles in order to have a city that is quieter, safer, and more neighborly. This decision must be made politically, because it is a decision about the public realm.

Within the framework of this political decision, people can also make individual decisions about how they want to live. Even in postwar America, where the political push was all for suburbia, there were some people who chose to stay in their old ethnic neighborhoods or to move from the suburbs to old inner-city neighborhoods that attracted bohemians because the rent and living expenses were low. Likewise, the city that you would get after putting political limits on automobile use would depend on people's individual preferences: the three models in Chapter 5 assumed that people preferred low densities, as most Americans do, but the cities would end up looking very different if people preferred urban neighborhoods, as most Europeans do.

People should make these decisions for themselves, because they are decisions about what sort of lives people want to live. The decision about limiting automobile use must be a political choice. The decision about what sort of housing to live in with any given transportation system should be an individual choice. These key decisions determining how a city is designed are not technical decisions that should be made by urban planners.

This does not mean that we should – or can – do without planning. Even with the most extreme limits on urban growth that we looked at in Chapter 5, planning is needed to lay out transportation routes, regional parks, utilities, and so on.

It does mean that we should subordinate planning to political and individual choices about how we want to live. Democratic decisions, such as the decision about what sort of transportation system we want to spend public funds on, and individual decisions, such as people's decisions about what sort of neighborhood they want to live in, should determine the big picture of how the city is designed. Planners should project the trends that result from these choices and should provide the transportation lines, regional parks, water systems, and other infrastructure needed to accommodate these choices.

If we put political limits on technology, we will put the planners in their proper place, useful but subordinate. We will also reduce the problems that the planners have to solve to a manageable level, making it possible for the planners to deal with these problems successfully.

Our thinking about technological decisions has already begun to change.

When city planners built freeways during the 1950s, everyone believed that the decision about whether a freeway was needed was a technical problem, which the planners should decide by doing studies of projected demand. But when some city planners began to oppose freeway construction during the 1960s, they talked about the freeways' effects on the "quality of life." By asking this qualitative question, this question about whether we want to live in cities built around freeways, they turned the decision about whether the freeway was needed into a political question that should be decided democratically.

Likewise, the New Urbanists have made decisions about urban designs more democratic by holding charettes where people in a community make decisions about neighborhood design by looking at drawings and computer visualizations of alternative designs. They have found that people react very differently when they are shown designs visually than when they are told about the same designs in abstract terms, as a given number of units built at a given density. When proposals are presented as an abstraction, people are more likely to be against density, but when the same proposals are presented visually, people are more likely to think that a shopping street looks more friendly and livable with a couple of stories of housing added above the stores.

Both of these examples show that looking at urban design in concrete, human terms does not mean ignoring the planners. City planners were among the first to talk about limiting freeway construction, because they were the first to learn the facts about the subject. But there was a big difference between the city planners who built the freeways, who wanted to solve technical transportation problems for a passive public, and the city planners who opposed the freeways by talking about their effect on the quality of life, a human question that turned freeway construction into a political issue. Likewise, the urban designers who run charettes allow ordinary people to make sensible decisions about urban design by converting the abstractions that planners deal with into concrete visual terms, so people can decide which is the sort of city they want to live in.

When we stop thinking about cities as bundles of technical problems and start thinking about cities qualitatively, about the different ways we live in different types of cities, then we will be able to act as citizens who use the law to govern ourselves – not as clients who expect the planners to provide us with more housing, more transportation, and a better environment.

The Failure of Growth

Why did our thinking about technology and growth change so dramatically during the twentieth century? Early in the century, everyone thought it was inevitable that the planners would gain more power because they were competent to mobilize technology and maximize growth. Today, almost everyone agrees that we need some control on technology and growth: the idea that we need planning to control the destructive side-effects of growth has become a commonplace, and this book's call for direct political limits on urban growth carries the same bias one step further.

This change occurred during the twentieth century because we moved from a scarcity economy to a surplus economy.

In late nineteenth century, the average American lived at what we now define as the poverty level, and new technology was increasing production income rapidly. This is the economic situation that gave birth to the technocratic theories of Thorstein Veblen and the early functionalist architects. When America desperately needed more economic growth to eliminate widespread poverty, people were willing to give power to the technocrats who could engineer growth.

In the late nineteenth century, for example, urban workers in the United States lived in over-crowded tenements, where the inner rooms had no windows and where all the apartments on a floor shared one toilet. The early functionalists drew up plans for mass produced "workers housing" that used new technology to provide everyone with housing that met basic standards of decency. No one objected that the housing was impersonal and monotonous; the important thing was that people had enough living space, a private bathroom, some sun shining into the windows, and somewhere for the children to play – because those basics were enough to make this housing an immense improvement over the tenements.

In the twentieth century, most Americans emerged from poverty. In 2000, America's per capita GDP was more than seven times as much as it was in 1900 (after correcting for inflation).[134] Because of increasing affluence, twentieth century America was very successful at producing housing for the masses – with Levittown as the archetypal mass-produced suburb. In America today, the masses live in suburban subdivisions and own two cars per family – and many have trouble keeping up with the payments. They have the basics that the technocrats planned for a century ago – a private bathroom, sun shining into the windows, lawns where the children can play – and they are forced to go so far beyond the basics that they are economically stressed: their neighborhoods are designed so they cannot buy groceries or get a cup of coffee without driving. Their lives would be easier if they had the choice of living in neighborhoods where they could get by with one car, or even with none, rather than needing two.

One hundred years ago, it made some sense to let the planners make the decisions about what should be produced. In a scarcity economy, where the way to improve people's well-being was by using technology to increase production, it was plausible to give decision-making power to the planners who could mobilize technology effectively.

Today, it no longer makes sense to let the planners make the decisions for us. Now that the average American has the necessities and many extras, we need to think critically about the human purposes of the economy. The goals of production are no longer as obvious as they were when most people did not have adequate housing. Rather than deciding how to produce basic, decent housing most efficiently, which is a technical question for housers and other planners to answer, we have to decide what types of neighborhoods we want to live in, which is a human question for everyone to answer.

The Rise and Fall of the Suburbs

We can see the failure of growth very clearly by looking at the history of the middle-class neighborhoods of American cities. During most of American history, growth made neighborhoods more livable, but during recent decades, growth has made our neighborhoods less livable.

Before the nineteenth century, all large cities were built as "walking cities."[135] Because most people got around by foot, cities had to be very dense. People lived in three to six story buildings, in row houses and apartments, often with shopping on the ground level. Streets were narrow, and buildings were not set back from the sidewalk. The older parts of European cities and towns are still built this way, and some early American cities were just as intense: the streets of eighteenth century Philadelphia looked like the streets of London, though there were vast areas of open land nearby.

Beginning early in the nineteenth century, steam-powered ferries and horse-drawn omnibuses let the American middle class live at lower densities. New neighborhoods typically had residential streets made up of three-story row houses: streets were wider, and houses were set back a few feet from the sidewalk and had larger backyards. Houses were commonly built on one-twentieth acre lots.

Beginning late in the nineteenth century, horsecars on steel tracks, cable cars, and electric trolley cars let the middle class move to "streetcar suburbs,"[136] which we think of today as classic American neighborhoods. They were made up of free-standing houses, with fairly large backyards, small front yards, and front porches looking out on tree-lined streets. Houses were commonly built on one-tenth-acre lots.

Streetcar suburbs felt spacious and quiet, but their most important form of transportation was still walking, though they were only about one-tenth the density of the traditional walking city. Streetcars were used for commuting to work and for occasional trips to other parts of town, but everyone lived within walking distance of a neighborhood shopping street.

Many people like cities, but for those who prefer the suburbs, new transportation technology and economic growth brought real benefits during the nineteenth and early twentieth century. From the walking city, to the row-house neighborhood, to the streetcar suburb, middle-class neighborhoods became greener, quieter, more spacious, healthier, safer for children.

During the twentieth century, Americans moved to even lower density suburbs. After World War I, middle-class neighborhoods were made up of bungalows on one-sixth acre lots: often, the neighborhood stores were not quite close enough to walk to easily, so people drove a few blocks on local streets to buy their groceries. After World War II, middle-class neighborhoods were made up of suburban homes on quarter-acre lots: the city was rebuilt around the freeway, and you had to drive on high speed arterial streets, where the traffic was nerve racking, to buy your groceries.

During the twentieth century, the middle-class moved from one-tenth acre lots in streetcar suburbs where you can walk to quarter-acre lots in postwar suburbs where you have to drive.

Yet all the extra land that we consumed during the twentieth century did not make neighborhoods more livable. All the automobiles made neighborhoods noisier, more congested, and less safe for children. The nearby farmland and open space that attracted people to suburbia was paved over, replaced by more freeways, strip malls and tract housing. The sense of community disappeared, as local shopping streets were replaced by regional shopping centers.

Likewise, all the extra transportation that we consumed – the freeways and the two or more family cars – did not make it more convenient for us to get around. As we have seen, research has shown that the amount of time that Americans spend commuting and budget to transportation tends to remain constant.[137] As speeds increased, suburbs sprawled, and malls got bigger, and people drove further to get to their jobs or to go shopping.

The middle class did become much larger during the twentieth century. One hundred years ago, most Americans were working class, and only a minority could afford to live in streetcar suburbs. Families generally considered themselves better off when postwar prosperity expanded the middle class and let them move from urban apartments to Levittown – but they would also have been better off if they had moved from apartments to streetcar suburbs.

Lower densities stopped improving neighborhoods during the twentieth century. Neighborhoods became more livable as middle class Americans moved from the walking city, to row houses, to streetcar suburbs. But by World War I, the middle class was already living in neighborhoods that were adequate. The streetcar suburbs gave families enough space, enough privacy, enough quiet, a big enough yard. Modern suburbia does not bring much added benefit, but it does cause real social and environmental problems, such as air pollution, automobile accidents, congestion, loss of open space, the ugliness of shopping malls and strips, and now global warming. At some time during the twentieth century, we reached the point where the costs of urban growth outweighed its benefits.

Limiting Noise

Noise is another telling example of the failure of growth. All through the nineteenth and twentieth century, the middle class tried to move to quieter neighborhoods by moving to lower density suburbs. Until World War I, they succeeded: from the walking city to the streetcar suburb, middle-class neighborhoods did become pleasanter and quieter. But during the twentieth century, so many new sources of noise appeared that modern suburbia is noisier than the much denser streetcar suburbs were one hundred years ago.

It should be obvious by now that the only way to reduce noise is by limiting its sources.

For example, cities and suburbs could cut their noise levels significantly by banning gasoline-powered gardening equipment. Electric edgers and electric chain saws work just as well, and there are always electrical outlets within reach on urban or suburban lots; there are also rechargeable battery-powered lawn mowers available. Some cities already have banned gasoline powered leaf blowers, because people refuse to put up with this new nuisance; the next step is to go back and get rid of the old nuisances that people accepted in the days when they thought less about the quality of life.

Some sources of noise can be banned at the municipal level, but we also need strict Federal standards to limit noise from motorcycles, garbage trucks, construction equipment, trucks with refrigeration equipment, and the like. Federal noise standards were developed in the 1970s, but they were never implemented, because the Reagan administration said they would slow economic growth: no doubt Reagan believed that people needed faster growth so they could afford to move to suburbia and get away from the city's noise.

Likewise, if we want any quiet in our parks, we need to restrict the use of jet skis, snowmobiles, off-road vehicles and other motorized recreational equipment. Americans already spend too much time pushing buttons and getting instant gratification, and we would be better off with outdoor recreation that requires more physical effort, such as canoeing, sailing, hiking, and bicycling. Environmentalists have had some success in banning off-road vehicles, snowmobiles, and jet skis.

Finally, if we want any quiet in either our cities or our countryside, we need quieter cars and trucks. Hybrid cars, such as the Toyota Prius, are much quieter than ordinary cars. Likewise, hybrid turbine buses reduce the noise and pollution from diesel buses dramatically, and we need similar technologies to replace conventional diesel trucks.

Vehicles are the single greatest source of noise in suburbs and cities. Noise is the number one reason that people give for wanting to live in lower density neighborhoods. Noise is also responsible for some of our worst suburban design – such as subdivisions surrounded by sound walls. There will be limits to the popularity of neotraditional neighborhoods until we do something to reduce traffic noise: many people will not want to live in denser neighborhoods if they have to listen to neighbors revving up their cars and motorcycles.

Noise is a clear example of the failure of growth. Through the nineteenth century, growth and new technology such as electric streetcars allowed people to escape from the cities to lower density neighborhoods that were quieter. During the twentieth century, new technology allowed people to escape to even lower density neighborhoods, but new technology also made these neighborhoods noisier. By now, it should be clear that political control of technology is needed to give us quiet neighborhoods or even a quiet countryside.

Urban Growth and Economic Growth

The failure of urban growth is just one part of a larger failure of economic growth. In fact, federal funding for freeways and guarantees for suburban mortgages were justified during the postwar period, precisely because they promoted economic growth by stimulating the auto industry and the construction industry. We have seen that consuming more transportation and more land for housing no longer makes our cities more livable. There is also reason to believe that economic growth generally has also stopped increasing our well being.

Several studies have developed indexes that measure America's economic well being, correcting the Gross Domestic Product by subtracting money that we spend to cope with problems caused by growth, such as the cost of pollution control technologies, and by subtracting an estimated money value of environmental costs that we live with, such as noise. In general, they have found that growth increased our well being until the 1960s or 1970s, and then growth began to reduce our well being.

The Daly-Cobb Index of Sustainable Economic Welfare, one of the earliest of these indexes, corrected the Gross National Product by subtracting the estimated money value of environmental costs and also subtracting extra spending on health care, education, commuting, and urbanization that is necessary only to support growth, which economists call "defensive expenditures." It also corrected for inequality of income. According to this index, Americans' economic well being increased substantially during the 1950s and 1960s, leveled off from 1968 until the end of the 1970s, and declined after 1980.[138]

The Genuine Progress Indicator, compiled by an organization named Redefining Progress, makes even more extensive corrections to the Gross Domestic Product. It shows that our actual economic well being rose until the early 1970s, then leveled off beginning in the late 1970s, so the average American has become no better off since the 1970s, despite our much higher per capita GDP.[139]

The economist Juliet Schor has shown that a significant number of Americans are now "downshifters," people who have deliberately chosen to consume less so they can work shorter hours and have more time to devote to their families and their other interests.[140] But there is a limit to how much individuals can downshift if they live in cities that burden them with the expense of driving every time they leave their homes. Downshifting could go much further if we also made political decisions that promoted it.

We tend to think about the larger issue of economic growth in the same way that we think about urban growth. Just as we consider the city a bundle of problems that must be solved by planners because they are too complex for ordinary people to deal with – transportation problems, housing problems, environmental problems, and the like – we also think of the economy as a bundle of problems that we must leave to the planners because they are too complex for us to deal with – inflation, unemployment, shortages of resources, global warming. We ignore the human question that underlies all these technical economic problems: how much we should consume to live a good life.

The three models in Chapter 5 look at the city and ask what level of consumption is enough to live a good life. We need to ask the same question about the entire economy: How much is enough?

This book has looked at ways that we can choose the sort of cities we live in, politically and individually, based on the sort of lives we want to lead, and it has shown that these choices can dramatically reduce the problems that urban planners need to deal with. The same is true of the entire economy: if we begin to choose our standard of living politically and individually, we can dramatically reduce problems such as resource shortages and global warming, making it more likely that our economic and environmental planners will be able to deal with these problems successfully.

The limits on urban growth that we looked at in this book are just one part of a larger change that is needed to move beyond the era of economic growth.

Citizens or Clients

The policies needed as the next steps toward rebuilding our cities are all politically feasible. Wisconsin requires cities to offer zoning choice. Freeway construction has virtually been ended in Great Britain because of political opposition. Many cities in America are reengineering streets to make them safer for pedestrians and are adding light rail or exclusive bus ways, and a few cities are removing freeways. Old downtowns are being revived, and the New Urbanists have begun replacing shopping centers and strip malls with old-fashioned neighborhoods.

There is enough support for these policies that they add up to a new political movement. Until recently, it was primarily a negative movement that tried to stop things from getting worse by fighting against freeways and sprawl. Today, it has become a positive movement that is making things better. Only one thing prevents it becoming a mass movement that changes our cities dramatically: everyone believes that changing our cities is a technical problem that must be left to the planners.

We still believe it is up to the planners to redesign our cities, as the technocrats claimed a century ago. Ordinary people are passive consumers of the services that the planners provide: the most they can do is demand more and better planning.

We believe it is up to the transportation planners to provide us with mobility. We ignore the fact that the average American drives twice as much now as in the 1960s and is no better off as a result of all this extra mobility. Instead, we stick with the old technocratic idea that it is up to the planners to deploy the technology that provides us with transportation. This technocratic approach implies that ordinary people are consumers who have no political responsibilities, and so it has drained us of the political will that we need to limit technology and make our cities livable.

It is revealing that we try to reduce traffic problems not by limiting the automobile but by subsidizing public transit. Our urban planners agree that Americans travel too much, that we need to build housing, work, and shopping near each other to reduce the need for transportation. But instead of reining in the automobile, we provide subsidies to mass transit in addition to the huge subsidies we give the automobile, though all these subsidies obviously cause us to travel longer distances. Our newer urban rail systems give a subsidy of over $10 per one-way trip to people who commute to the most remote suburbs, which comes to over $10,000 per year to a family with two commuters – and that only includes the operating subsidy, not the capital expenses.[141] With huge public subsidies to both commuter rail and the automobile, more people keep moving to suburbia, and traffic keeps getting worse.

This sort of thing will happens as long as people expect the planners to solve our problems. Rather than demanding that the planners provide us with more transportation, we need to realize that we would be better off with less transportation – and that the way to get there is by using the law to put direct limits on destructive forms of transportation.

The calls for more planning assume that centralized organizations staffed by experts should provide us with goods and services, and ordinary people are nothing more than consumers. This view made some sense one hundred years ago, when scarcity was the key economic problem, but it makes no sense now that over-consumption is the key economic problem in the United States and the other developed nations. Today, we need to invert this technocratic view, so we can change from clients who expect the planners to solve our problems into citizens who deal with these problems ourselves by putting direct political limits on destructive technologies and on growth.

Notes

[1] "Make no little plans. They have no magic to stir men's blood and probably themselves will not be realized. Make big plans; aim high in hope and work, remembering that a noble, logical diagram once recorded will never die, but long after we are gone will be a living thing, asserting itself with ever-growing insistency. Remember that our sons and grandsons are going to do things that would stagger us. Let your watchword be order and your beacon beauty. Think big." – Daniel Burnham

[2] Louis Sullivan was the first to say "Form follows function," and he did not want to eliminate all ornamentation, only to build structures that grew out of and did not hide their functions. Other theorists saw functionalism primarily as an esthetic doctrine; for example, see Henry-Russell Hitchcock, Jr., and Philip Johnson, Ed., *The International Style: Architecture Since 1922* (New York, W. W. Norton & Company, 1932). However, the dogmatic functionalists described here had the most effect on the theory of city planning.

[3] Alan Colquhoun, "Typology and Design Method" in Charles Jencks and George Baird, ed., *Meaning in Architecture* (New York, George Braziller, 1970) p. 268.

[4] Jacques Ellul, *The Technological Society*, John Wilkinson, trans. (New York, Alfred A. Knopf, 1964) p. 80. Ellul was a critic of technology, but he was also a pessimist who believed that nothing could be done to control technology.

[5] Thorstein Veblen, *The Engineers and the Price System* (New York, Viking Press, 1954, copyright 1921) p. 69.

[6] Thorstein Veblen, *Imperial Germany and the Industrial Revolution* (New York, Viking Press, 1954, copyright 1915) p. 270.

[7] Edward Bellamy, *Looking Backward: 2000-1887* (New York and Scarborough, Ontario, New American Library: Signet Classics, 1960) p. 58 *et seq.* Marx also talked about "industrial armies," meaning that workers would be drafted by the state, like soldiers, rather than hired by capitalists; he included "establishment of industrial armies" in his list of the key changes that communism would bring, at the end of section II of the Communist Manifesto. Karl Marx and Friedrich Engels, *The Communist Manifesto* (New York and London, Modern Reader Publications, 1968) p. 40.

[8] Veblen, *Engineers and the Price System*, p. 138 *et seq.*

[9] Veblen, *Engineers and the Price System*, p. 121.

[10] Veblen, *Engineers and the Price System*, p, 166.

[11] This is the theory, but the French planner Gaston Bardet pointed out that Le Corbusier's drawings of the Radiant City show the shadows buildings would cast at noon on June 21; at noon on December 21, the city of light would be a city of shadows. Gaston Bardet, *Pierre sur Pierre* (Paris, Edition L.C.B., 1945) p. 180.

[12] Charles Edouard Jeanneret-Gris (pseudonym: Le Corbusier), *Towards a New Architecture*, trans. Frederick Etchells (London, The Architectural Press, 1946) p. 122.

[13] Walter Gropius, *The New Architecture and the Bauhaus*, trans. P. Morton Shand and Joseph Hudnut (New York, Museum of Modern Art, and London, Faber & Faber Ltd., undated) p. 68 *et seq.*

[14] Walter Gropius, "Sociological Premises for the Minimum Dwelling of Urban Industrial Populations," in Walter Gropius, *Scope of Total Architecture* (New York, Harper & Bros., World Perspectives, 1955) p. 104.

[15] Quoted in Wolf Von Eckardt, *A Place to Live: The Crisis of the Cities* (New York, Delta Books, 1967) p. 90.

[16] Quoted in Von Eckardt, *A Place to Live,* p. 90.

[17] Sigfried Giedion, *Space, Time and Architecture: the Growth of a New Tradition* (Cambridge, Mass., Harvard University Press, 1954) p. 744.

[18] Giedion, *Space, Time and Architecture*, p. 707-708.

[19] Giedion, *Space, Time and Architecture*, p. 756.

[20] Giedion, *Space, Time and Architecture*, p. 722.

[21] Giedion, *Space, Time and Architecture*, p. 730.

[22] Quoted in Robert Fishman, *Urban Utopias in the Twentieth Century: Ebenezer Howard, Frank Lloyd Wright and Le Corbusier* (New York, Basic Books, 1977) p. 33.

[23] Sir Ebenezer Howard, *Garden Cities of Tomorrow*, F.J. Osborn, ed. (London, Faber & Faber, 1951).

[24] Lewis Mumford, *The Culture of Cities* (New York, Harcourt, Brace & Co., 1938) p. 296.

[25] Mumford, *Culture of Cities*, pp. 351-352.

[26] Lewis Mumford, *Technics and Civilization* (New York and Burlingame, Harcourt, Brace & World, 1963, first edition 1934) p. 417.

[27] Mumford, *Technics and Civilization*, p. 388.

[28] Mumford, *Culture of Cities*, caption to photograph on page following p. 435.

[29] Mumford, *Culture of Cities*, caption to photograph on page following p. 435.

[30] Mumford, *Culture of Cities*, caption to photograph on the page preceding p. 438.

[31] Benton MacKaye, *From Geography to Geotechnics*, Paul T. Bryan, ed., (Urbana, Ill., University of Illinois Press, 1968) p. 143-145.

[32] Mumford, *Culture of Cities*, p. 344.

[33] Henry Wright, *Rehousing Urban America* (New York, Columbia University Press, 1935) p. 24.

[34] Mumford, *Technics and Civilization*, caption to photograph on page preceding p. 373.

[35] For Mumford's changed view of technology after the atom bomb was dropped, see the 1948 essay about the atom bomb, "Miracle or Catastrophe" in Lewis Mumford, *In the Name of Sanity* (New York, Harcourt, Brace and Company, 1954), pp. 63-99, and see the 1948 essay "Technics and the Future of Western Civilization" in Mumford, *In the Name of Sanity*, pp. 34-62.

[36] Mumford, *Culture of Cities*, p. 458.

[37] Clarence Perry, *Housing for the Machine Age* (New York, Russell Sage Foundation, 1939) p. 51. Perry emphasized this point: "If any of the original boundaries of a unit are not suited for through traffic, they should be widened by taking land, if necessary, from the unit area."(Perry, *Housing for the Machine Age*, p. 56)

[38] "Wide and conspicuous boundaries enable residents and the public in general to see the limits of the community and visualize it as a distinct entity." Perry, *Housing for the Machine Age*, p. 472, p. 56-57.

[39] Perry, *Housing for the Machine Age*, see map on p. 54.

[40] Robert Ezra Park, *Human Communities: the City and Human Ecology* (Glencoe, Ill., The Free Press, 1952) pp. 240-241.

[41] Park, *Human Communities*, p. 230.

[42] Louis Wirth, "Human Ecology" in Richard Sennett, ed., *Classic Essays on the Culture of Cities* (New York, Appleton-Century-Crofts Educational Division: Meredith Corporation, 1969) p. 173.

[43] Published in *The American Journal of Sociology*, vol. xx, # 5, March, 1915, p 577- 612.

[44] Park, *Human Communities*, p. 16-17. The 1915 essay is rewritten as the first chapter of this book. It is unfortunate that Sennett reprinted this later version in *Classic Essays* (91 *et seq.*) but gave it the earlier date, giving the

impression city planning was far more advanced early in the century than was actually the case.

[45] Park, *Human Communities*, p. 41.

[46] Park, *Human Communities*, p. 32.

[47] Daniel Bell, *The End of Ideology: On the Exhaustion of Political Ideas in the 1950s* (Glencoe, Illinois, The Free Press, 1960).

[48] Quoted in Christopher Lasch, *The Culture of Narcissism: American Life in an Age of Diminishing Expectations* (New York, W.W. Norton & Co., 1978), p. 77.

[49] A national highway system was first proposed after a 1938 study by the Bureau of Public Roads led to a "Master Plan for Free Highway Development" that called for a 27,000 mile network of inter-regional highways, which would be limited access, would be elevated or depressed in urban areas, and would include inner and outer belt roads in cities to allow traffic to bypass central business districts. The 1952 and 1954 Federal Aid Highway Acts allocated $25 million and $175 million to build these roads, but this funding came out of general funds, and the acts were criticized for contributing to the federal budget deficit. The Federal Highway Act of 1956 increased the proposed length of the system to 41,000 miles and renamed it the National System of Interstate and Defense Highways. The Highway Revenue Act of 1956 created the Highway Trust Fund to pay the federal share of the cost of these roads and credited all revenue from the federal gasoline tax and other motor vehicle taxes to this fund. Today, the Interstate Highway System is 45,024 miles.

[50] Mark Hansen and Yuanlin Huang, "Road Supply and Traffic in Californian Urban Areas," *Transportation Research A*, Volume 31, No 3, 1997, pp. 205-218.

[51] UK Department of Transport, *Report of the Standing Committee on Trunk Road Assessment*, December 1994 and Guidance Document 24 L, based on this report.

[52] Jerome M. Segal, "What We Work for Now," *New York Times*, September 3, 2001, p. A19. Segal estimates that Americans spent 1 or 2% of their income on transportation a century ago, but he points out that we do not

know the exact amount, because it was so small that the census bureau did not consider transportation as a separate category at the time.

[53] Jane Holtz Kay, *Asphalt Nation: How the Automobile Took Over America and How We Can Take It Back* (New York, Crown Publishers, 1997) p. 121.

[54] Kay, *Asphalt Nation*, p. 124.

[55] Jean Gottmann, *Megalopolis: The Urbanized Northeastern Seaboard of the United States* (Cambridge, Mass., MIT Press, 1961) p. 652.

[56] Kay, *Asphalt Nation*, p. 346.

[57] Quoted in Kenneth Jackson, *Crabgrass Frontier: The Suburbanization of the United States* (New York, Oxford University Press, 1985) p. 195.

[58] Jackson, *Crabgrass Frontier*, p. 196.

[59] David Gebhard *et al.*, *A Guide to Architecture in San Francisco and Northern California* (Santa Barbara, Peregrine Smith Inc., 1973) p. 109.

[60] Martin Anderson, *The Federal Bulldozer* (Cambridge, Mass., MIT Press, 1964) p. 75.

[61] Herbert J. Gans, *The Levittowners: Ways of Life and Politics in a New Suburban Community* (New York, Pantheon Books: division of Random House, 1967) p. 36-40.

[62] Robert Caro, *The Power Broker: Robert Moses and the Fall of New York* (New York, Alfred A. Knopf, 1974) pp. 341-344.

[63] Robert Goodman, *After the Planners* (New York, Simon & Schuster, 1971) p. 74.

[64] Jackson, *Crabgrass Frontier*, p. 197-198.

[65] Quoted in Goodman, *After the Planners*, p. 58.

[66] Buzz Bissinger, *A Prayer for the City* (New York, Random House, 1997) p. 207.

[67] Jackson, *Crabgrass Frontier*, p. 203.

[68] Jane Jacobs, *The Death and Life of Great American Cities* (New York, Random House: Vintage Books, 1961) p. 300.

[69] Jacobs, *Death and Life*, p. 306-307.

[70] Oscar Newman, *Defensible Space: Crime Prevention through Urban Design* (New York, Macmillan, 1972). Though there have been criticisms of the methodology of this book, its basic thesis that modernist housing projects increased crime is indisputable.

[71] The official population of the project was 20,000 people, but it was estimated that an additional 5,000 to 7,000 residents were not registered with the housing authority. This is less than 1% of Chicago's population, but in 1980, 11% of Chicago's murders, 9% of rapes, and 10% of aggravated assaults occurred in this project. William Julius Wilson, *The Truly Disadvantaged: The Inner City, the Underclass, and Public Policy* (Chicago, University of Chicago Press, 1990) p. 25.

[72] Peter Calthorpe and William Fulton, *The Regional City: Planning for the End of Sprawl* (Washington, Covelo, London, Island Press, 2001) p. 245.

[73] Fannie Mae (Federal National Mortgage Association) buys mortgages from banks, giving a fresh supply of capital to the banks that make the mortgage loans, and it focuses almost exclusively on single family housing, rather than on the multifamily housing and mixed-use projects (with housing above shopping) that are often needed in cities. In 1998, only 1.4% of Fannie Mae's purchases went to multifamily housing, and zero went to mixed use projects. Calthorpe and Fulton, *The Regional City*, p. 97.

[74] Victor Gruen, *Centers for the Urban Environment* (New York, Van Nostrand Reinhold, 1973) p. 53.

[75] Jacobs, *Death and Life*, p. 170.

[76] Jacobs, *Death and Life*, p. 152 *et seq.*

[77] Jacobs, *Death and Life*, p. 154 -156.

[78] Courts in California, Oregon, Massachusetts, Colorado, Washington, and New Jersey have ruled that there should be some protection for free speech

in shopping malls, but there is no protection in the other states.

[79] Gruen, *Centers*, p. 87.

[80] Unfortunately, Gruen's designs for these "multi-functional centers" kept many of the features he learned by developing shopping centers: Gruen designed loop freeways and peripheral parking lots around downtown areas to keep them free of traffic, but these act as boundaries which discourage people in nearby neighborhoods from walking to downtown. His most famous design was his plan for Fort Worth, Texas, which would have surrounded a downtown of about one square mile with a ring road feeding into six parking garages that held ten thousand cars each. Downtown itself would have been kept free of automobiles and developed more intensively as a mixed use area. This plan essentially would have turned downtown into an immense regional shopping mall (albeit a mixed-use rather than a single-use mall), integrating downtown into the automotive scale of the region as a whole. But despite its flaws, Gruen's work does show clearly that functional land-use planning is a major cause of the need for transportation planning.

[81] In one sign of how important he was considered at the time, Wolf Von Eckert, the architecture critic of the Washington Post, wrote a popularized version of Gottmann's book *Megalopolis*, summarizing its points in a shorter text with more illustrations to capture a wider audience. Wolf Von Eckert, *The Challenge of Megalopolis: a Graphic Presentation of the Urbanized Northeastern Seaboard of the United States* (New York, Macmillan, 1964).

[82] "Witness, for example, the impact of the Federal government in Washington, D.C., as it tightens up over many aspects of national life, the continued crowding of financial and managerial operations into Manhattan; New York's dominance of the national market for mass-communication media ..., and the preeminent influence of the universities and cultural centers of Megalopolis ...." Gottmann, *Megalopolis*, p. 8.

[83] For example, he said about traffic congestion: "there is a constant threat that means of transportation , . . will become inadequate; and a constantly greater part of what ought to be leisure time is spent traveling ... from home to work, from work to home, to places of recreation and so forth." Gottmann, *Megalopolis*, p. 247. He said about sprawl, "So many communities have been growing close to one another that they often run short of space." Gottmann, *Megalopolis*, p. 727. He wrote when the cities between Boston

and Washington were first turning into a continuous metropolitan area, without open countryside separating them.

[84] Gottmann, *Megalopolis*, p. 776.

[85] Gottmann, *Megalopolis*, p. 632.

[86] Gottmann, *Megalopolis*, p. 247.

[87] Consider how New York City's freeway system was developed. From the 1930's through the 1950's, virtually all of the New York metropolitan area's highway planning and much of its urban planning was under the control of Robert Moses. In 1933, when Mayor LaGuardia offered him a position as City Parks commissioner, Moses answered, "I was not interested in taking the job unless I had unified control over all the city's parks and, even then, only as part of the system of parks and parkway development." (Caro, *Power Broker*, p. 360). By 1934 Moses headed all seven governmental agencies concerned with New York's parks and parkways. (*ibid.*, p, 362) By the end of World War II, Moses held twelve city and state positions. He not only was in charge of parks and highways, but as head of the Mayor's Slum Clearance committee (*ibid.*, p, 707) controlled New York's urban renewal programs. He also effectively controlled the City Planning commission (*ibid.*, p, 742) and Housing Authority (*ibid.*, p, 706), though he had no formal connection with these agencies.

He used these powers to rebuild much of Manhattan in the "great scale," of the freeway and the single-function superblocks. He demolished acre after acre of slum apartments and replaced them with superblocks of towers-in-a-park housing for the middle class and the poor – many overlooking the Henry Hudson Parkway and Harlem River Drive, both of which he had built. This is as close as any individual in America has ever come to building the modernists' ideal city. Moses' work was admired by modernist planning theorists: for example, Sigfried Giedion said that Moses' freeways "will constitute the forerunner of the city on a new scale." (Giedion, *Space, Time and Architecture*, p. 735.)

In all, Moses constructed 627 miles of super-highways in and around New York City, (Peter Blake, *Form Follows Fiasco*, Boston and Toronto, Little Brown, 1977, p. 106.) the majority of highways and bridges in the region. Moses was an adamant foe of mass transit: he deliberately built the overpasses of his parkways so low that buses could not use the roads. (Caro, *Power Broker*, p. 318).

Moses had also worked with the Eisenhower administration in planning the Interstate Highway System, which dominates American transportation today. The scope of the system's funding, $50 billion to construct 41,000 miles of highways, was Moses' idea. One of the early managers, and the de facto head, of the Interstate System was Bertram D. Tallamy, who had attended a series of private lectures that Moses had given in 1926, and who said that the system was built according to the principles he had learned at those lectures (Caro, *Power Broker*, p, 706). Immediately after the Interstate Highway Act had passed, Moses was ready to present Washington with a proposal for a complete system of highways joining New York and New Jersey with highways in other states (Caro, *Power Broker*, pp, 921-922).

Given this history, it is hard to believe Gottmann can claim that Megalopolis' dependence on the automobile results from a lack of centralized planning.

[88] Gottmann, *Megalopolis*, p. 738.

[89] Gottmann, *Megalopolis*, p. 247.

[90] Quoted in Fishman, *Urban Utopias*, p. 35.

[91] Quoted in Daniel Bell, *The Coming of Post-Industrial Society* (New York, Basic Books, 1973) p. 31-33.

[92] Steffans actually said "I have been over into the future, and it works" when he returned from the Soviet Union in 1921, but the statement was widely quoted in the form "I've seen the future, and it works." This form of the quote was used by his wife, Ella Winter, on the title page of her book *Red Virtue*. Ella Winter, *Red Virtue: Human Relationships in the New Russia* (New York, Harcourt Brace & Co, 1933).

[93] Herbert Simon, *Administrative Behavior: A Study of Decision-Making Processes in Administrative Organizations*, third edition (New York, The Free Press, a division of Macmillan, 1976) p, 295.

[94] Benton MacKaye, *From Geography to Geotechnics*, Paul T. Bryant, ed. (Urban, Ill., University of Illinois Press, 1968) p. 59.

[95] It seems that the only people who still believe in the older notion of regionalism are romantic ecologists who call themselves "bio-regionalists," and who want to replace the older political boundaries with boundaries that correspond to the distribution of biological communities. But the

boundaries of bio-regions are different from the boundaries we would establish to form the sort of self-sufficient economic regions that the early planners called for. The bio-regionalists are just merely treating their own particular concern as if it were universal. They want planning to protect bio-diversity, and so they want to treat the boundaries that correspond to the habitat of species as if they were the only basis for planning – ignoring economic planning and transportation planning, for example.

[96] For example, Mumford summarized his program in *Technics and Civilization* in four sections in the imperative, each ending with an exclamation point: Increase Conversion! Economize Production! Normalize Consumption! and Socialize Creation! The section named "Normalize Consumption!" says the planners should establish norms of consumption so there is not endless growth: "… once the major wants of mankind are satisfied by the machine process, our factory system must be organized on the basis of regular annual replacement instead of progressive expansion." Mumford, *Technics and Civilization*, p. 397.

[97] Gottmann, *Megalopolis*, p 685.

[98] For his argument that "A network of small interconnected streets has more traffic capacity than the same street area arranged in a sparse hierarchy of large streets," see Walter Kulash "Traditional Neighborhood Development: Will the Traffic Work?" presentation at the 11th Annual Pedestrian Conference in Bellevue WA, October 1990, not published in print but available at http://user.gru.net/domz/kulash.htm.

[99] For a description and illustrations of this proposal, see Peter Katz, *The New Urbanism: Toward an Architecture of Community* (New York, McGraw-Hill, 1994) pp. 164-168.

[100] "We stand for the restoration of existing urban centers and towns within coherent metropolitan regions, the reconfiguration of sprawling suburbs into communities of real neighborhoods and diverse districts, the conservation of natural environments, and the preservation of your built legacy." The Charter of the New Urbanism, quoted in Calthorpe and Fulton, *The Regional City*, p. 282.

[101] ERE Yarmouth and Real Estate Research Corporation (RERC), *Emerging Trends in Real Estate, 1998* (Real Estate Research Corporation, Chicago, 1997) p. 24.

[102] See Andres Duany, Elizabeth Plater-Zyberk, and Jeff Speck, *Suburban Nation: The Rise of Sprawl and the Decline of the American Dream* (New York, Northpoint Press: a division of Farrar, Straus and Giroux, 2000) p. 176-178.

[103] Quoted in Allen R. Myerson, "What's New in Concert Halls? A Taste for the Old" *New York Times*, May 12, 1998, Section E, Page 2, Column 3. For more information about the redevelopment of downtown Fort Worth's Sundance Square, see Gregory Kallenberg "Downtown Fort Worth: Where Restoration and Building Is a Family Affair" *New York Times*, May 19, 1996, Section 9, Page 11, Column 1.

[104] James Brooke, "Denver Stands Out in Trend Toward Living in Downtown," *New York Times*, December 29, 1998, p. A1.

[105] For an overview of regional planning in the United States, see Calthorpe and Fulton, *Regional City*, pp. 105-171 and 185-194.

[106] The plan gave localities some flexibility about how to design this transit-oriented development. Towns had the choice of adopting the plan's standard zoning or of developing local zoning that would meet the plan's targets for housing and job growth.

[107] Information about Portland is from Calthorpe and Fulton, *Regional City*, pp. 107-125.

[108] *Wall Street Journal*, Dec. 26, 1995, p. 1.

[109] Alan Ehrenhalt, "New Recruits in the War on Sprawl," *New York Times*, April 13, 1999.

[110] "Metro's research found that one of the key variables for more walkable and transit-friendly environments was the frequency of street intersections. More frequent intersections allowed more direct foot and bike routes on local streets. With a more finely grained street network, local trips by car can easily stay on local streets – leaving the arteries free for through trips. This simple requirement for a denser street network helps reduce local congestion and directs development toward a more walkable form." Calthorpe and Fulton, *The Regional City*, p. 123.

[111] Figures from the Safe Routes to School National Partnership, http://www.saferoutespartnership.org/.

[112] Booth Tarkington, *Seventeen: A Tale of Youth and Summertime and the Baxter Family Especially William* (New York, Harper Brothers, 1932).

[113] In 1960, Americans drove 4,009 miles per capita, and in 2000, Americans drove 9,761 miles per capita. Susan B. Carter *et al.*, editors, *Historical Statistics of the United States: Earliest Times to the Present* (New York, Cambridge University Press, 2006), VMT figures from pp. 4-835 to 4-836, population figures from p. 1-26.

[114] Yacov Zahavi, *Travel Over Time*, Report PL-79-004 (FHWA, U.S. Department of Transportation, 1979). Yacov Zahavi and Antti Talvitie, "Regularities in Travel Time and Money Expenditures," *Transportation Research Record 750* (TRB, National Research Council, Washington, D.C. 1980) pp. 13-19. Yacov Zahavi and J. M. Ryan, "Stability of Travel Components Over Time," *Transportation Research Record 750* (TRB, National Research Council, Washington, D.C., 1980) pp. 19-26. A later study updated Zahavi's analysis using data through 1990 and concluded that he was right to say that people have a constant time budget that they devote to traveling: Gary Barnes and Gary Davis, *Land Use and Travel Choices in the Twin Cities, 1958 – 1990*. Report No. 6 in the series *Transportation and Regional Growth* (Minneapolis: Center for Transportation Studies, 2001).

[115] J. M. McLynn and Spielberg, "Procedures for Demand Forecasting Subject to Household Budget Constraints" in *Directions to Improve Travel Demand Forecasting: Conference Summary and White Papers*, HHP-22 (Washington DC, Federal Highway Administration, 1978) pp. 115-197.

[116] J. M. Ryan and B. D. Spear, "Directions toward the Better Understanding of Transportation and Urban Structure," in *Directions to Improve Travel Demand Forecasting*, pp. 199-247.

[117] Approximately 58% of the funding for Federal Highway Administration programs under the ISTEA (1992-1997) and TEA-21 (1998-2003) laws was flexible funding, which could be used for either highways or public transportation. But of this amount, the states spent only 5.6% on public transportation and the rest on highways. "Flexing To Transit: Are State Leaders as Flexible on Transit as Federal Law?" (no author given), *Surface Transportation Policy Project Progress*, vol. 12, number 2, October 2002.

[118] For example, *Construction News* wrote "like it or not, the industry has to concede – temporarily at least – that the anti-road lobby is winning

the battle over the desirability or otherwise of new roads. What used to be dismissed as Nimbyism is now a nationwide movement opposed to further large-scale road building, and the government appears to be taking note." Likewise, *Leader in Building – The Voice of the Industry* wrote, "Counting on the major roads projects is about as futile as the canal builders' resistance to the coming of the railways ... voters do not want more roads. As has long been expected, road traffic ... simply expands to fill the void created by bigger and better roads. The Roads to Prosperity culture is dead." Quoted in *Alarm Bells*, the newsletter of ALARM UK, issue 20, 1997.

[119] Department of the Environment, 1998a, *A New Deal for Transport: Better for Everyone*, TSO, London. See also, DETR, 1994, Guidance on Induced Traffic, Guidance Note 1/95, HETA Division, 14 December 1994.

[120] DETR, 2000, Transport 2010: The 10 Year Plan, TSO, London (www.detr.gov.uk/trans2010/index.htm).

[121] Wolfgang Zuckermann, *End of the Road: From World Car Crisis to Sustainable Transportation* (Post Mills, Vermont, Chelsea Green, 1992) p. 141.

[122] The Merry Hill shopping center reduced the number of shoppers by 70% at the nearby Dudley town center and 20 to 40% at other town centers, such as Stourbridge and West Bromwich.

[123] Congress for the New Urbanism, *The Coming Demand*, based on research by Dowell Myers, Elizabeth Gearin, Tridib Bannerjee, and Ajay Garde, University of Southern California School of Policy, Planning and Development (San Francisco, Congress for the New Urbanism, undated).

[124] For a number of examples of failed shopping malls that have been rebuilt as traditional neighborhoods, see Congress for the New Urbanism and PricewaterhouseCoopers, *Greyfields into Goldfields: From Failing Shopping Centers to Great Neighborhoods* (San Francisco, Congress for the New Urbanism, 2001)

[125] For a description and illustrations of this proposal, see Peter Katz, *The New Urbanism,* pp. 169-177.

[126] Vermont is the first state to be influenced by the ITE's New Urbanist road design standards. The battle over road design came to a head in Bethel,

Vermont, where the state's Agency of Transportation planned to replace a lightly traveled one-lane bridge between two narrow country roads with a new forty-foot wide bridge. Cheryl Rivers, a member of Bethel's Select Board, led the fight to stop this bridge and then won election to the State Senate, where she introduced the nation's strongest highway design reform law. Three of the Agency of Transportation's senior traffic engineers, who resisted the change, retired after this law passed in 1996.

[127] "Some Urban Planners Say Downtowns Need a Lot More Congestion" *Wall Street Journal*, Aug. 7, 1996, p. 1.

[128] For example, Kulash worked to make Wabasha St., in St. Paul, Minnesota, into a pedestrian-friendly main street. The Mayor of St. Paul, Norm Coleman, said that when the traffic engineers redesigned the city's streets in the 1960's, "moving traffic was their goal" but the new street patterns were "inextricably tied to urban decline" (*ibid.*, p 16) because they made downtown's streets so unattractive that no one wanted to walk there. With Kulash as a consultant, the city decided to replace a traffic lane on Wabasha St. with parking, to add street trees, and to consider making the street two-way again. Likewise, Wellesley, Massachusetts, rejected a plan to widen Route 16 and speed traffic through the center of town, and instead it decided to narrow the road and widen its sidewalks. Riverside and San Bernardino, California, have narrowed their main downtown streets from four lanes to two. Most dramatically, West Palm Beach, Florida improved its depressed downtown, which traffic used to speed through, by widening sidewalks and adding speed tables, humps and circles to slow drivers down. It also added a fountain, benches, and a public amphitheater used for city celebrations. These improvements attracted new private development to the area, and lowered vacancy rates that had been as high as 50%. (Source: Local Government Commission.)

[129] No author given, "More Evidence that Low Speeds Mean Clean Air," *T&E Bulletin: News from the European Federation for Transport and Environment*, No. 148, May 2006, p. 1.

[130] For histories of these freeway removals, see www.preservenet.com/ freeways.

[131] See note 4.

[132] By contrast, modern architects considered themselves experts who were competent to dictate how their clients live. Frank Lloyd Wright and Le

Corbusier were famous examples, and the designers of public housing projects did the same thing.

[133] One common argument for regional government is that it could allow revenue sharing. Taxes could be collected regionally and distributed to municipal governments, so poorer cities would get a larger share of taxes and land-use decisions would not be distorted by cities' competition for development and the tax dollars that go with it. In fact, we need a more radical scheme that replaces the sales tax and property tax with "green taxes," such as higher gasoline taxes and taxes on electricity that depend on the amount of carbon dioxide released to generate the electricity. Instead of taxing goods, such as housing and retail sales, we should tax "bads," such as pollution and carbon dioxide emissions. Though it may make sense to tax McMansions and the purchase of some luxury goods, it makes no sense at all to tax working people's housing and purchases of clothing – and it is an unfortunate historical fact that cities depend on property and sales taxes for most of their revenues. They should be replaced by green taxes, collected centrally and distributed to cities.

[134] In 1900, America's per capita GDP was $5,557 in 2005 dollars. In 2000, America's per capita GDP was $39,750 in 2005 dollars. Louis D. Johnston and Samuel H. Williamson, "The Annual Real and Nominal GDP for the United States, 1790 – Present," MeasuringWorth, 2008. www.measuringworth.org.

[135] Kenneth T. Jackson, *Crabgrass Frontier*, pp. 14-20.

[136] See Sam B. Warner, Jr., *Streetcar Suburbs: The Process of Growth in Boston, 1870-1900* (Cambridge, Mass., Harvard University Press and the MIT Press, 1962).

[137] See notes 114 and 115.

[138] Herman E. Daly and John B. Cobb, Jr., *For the Common Good: Redirecting the Economy Toward Community, the Environment, and a Sustainable Future* (Boston, Beacon Press, 1989) pp. 401-455. Because it is an older study, this index is based on the GNP rather than the GDP.

[139] The genuine progress indicator is available at http://www.rprogress.org/sustainability_indicators/genuine_progress_indicator.htm. For general background about the economic issues involved, see Clifford Cobb, Ted

Halstead, and Jonathan Rowe, "If the GDP is Up, Why is America Down?" *Atlantic Monthly*, October, 1995.

[140] Juliet B. Schor, *The Overspent American: Upscaling, Downshifting, and the New Consumer* (New York, Basic Books, 1998) p. 111 *et seq.*

[141] For example, on BART (the commuter rail system in the San Francisco Bay Area), the fare to San Francisco from the remote suburban station Dublin/Pleasanton is $5.55. Assuming that one-third of the total cost is recovered from the fare box, there is a subsidy of $11.10 per trip. In addition, parking is subsidized by at BART, and virtually all the riders at this suburban station drive to BART, while less than one-half of all passengers drive to BART, increasing the subsidy to suburban riders even further.

Made in the USA
Charleston, SC
12 April 2010